My Parents Never Had Sex

Golden Age Books

Perspectives on Aging

The Age of Aging: A Reader in Social Gerontology
edited by Abraham Monk

Caring for an Aging Parent: Have I Done All I Can?
by Avis Jane Ball

Handle With Care: A Question of Alzheimer's
by Dorothy S. Brown

Understanding "Senility": A Layperson's Guide
by Virginia Fraser and Susan M. Thornton

You, Your Parent, and the Nursing Home
by Nancy Fox

My Parents Never Had Sex

Myths and Facts of Sexual Aging

Doris B. Hammond, Ph.D.

PROMETHEUS BOOKS
Buffalo, New York

Cover Photo: The author and publisher wish to express their gratitude to Walt and Candy Parnell for permission to reprint the cover photograph. Mr. and Mrs. Parnell are shown with their two daughters, Heather and Jennifer. The Parnell family resides in Coral Springs, Florida.

Published 1987 by Prometheus Books
700 East Amherst Street, Buffalo, New York 14215

Library of Congress Cataloging Number: 87-20818

ISBN 0-87975-409-5 (Cloth)
0-87975-413-3 (Paper)

Dedication

To my wonderful and loving parents
who must have had sex—once,
and to my three daughters who know that I
had sex—thrice,
and to my husband, Ted—
who knows better!

Preface

My parents never had sex, did yours? Of course not! If we were really being honest with ourselves we would prefer to think that our births resulted from immaculate conceptions. We do seem to have a difficult time thinking of parents and grandparents as the sexual beings they really are. Why is that? This book may help children and grandchildren to understand and accept the sexuality of their elders and, in so doing, help to generate in each of us the self-understanding and self-acceptance we need as sexual beings.

How did a nice, middle-aged lady like me get so involved in sex? Well, as they say, somebody had to do it! Actually, that is true to a great extent. A graduate human sexuality course I took at the University of Georgia in the 1970s made me realize how little is really known about our total sexuality. Since I was taking many courses related to aging, I was encouraged to write my research paper on sexuality and aging, which led to a dissertation on the same topic. At that time there was little written about the sexuality of older people. One of the few books, and my "favorite," is titled *Sex After Sixty* and, guess what, all the pages are blank! I often use the book to begin audience presentations. Another favorite book of mine is *Eugenics: The Science of Hu man Life*, published in 1915. There are quotes from this book serving as epigrams at the beginning of each chapter.

What began as a tentative look at a very sensitive subject, about which I was no more comfortable than others of my generation, has developed into a topic with which I feel totally at ease. That's as it should be, and I hope this book will help others to develop that same comfortable feeling. I admit that, on occasion, when dining out and someone asks me about my sex research, my husband has to ask me not to talk so loud because, like E. F. Hutton, suddenly there is dead silence and all ears are listening.

I have received much encouragement from others in writing this book. My students at D'Youville College, Buffalo, New York, are especially excited and have been so helpful in sharing their many comments and experiences with me. My daughters, Kim, Darcy, and Lauri, and son-in-law, Carl, really think it's great. Well, I think they're pretty great! In fact, the first half of this book was written at my favorite "hide-away," Kim and Carl's home in South Carolina. My lovable mother is proud of her daughter's book, but I'm not sure she's told her friends what it's about. I remember the time she and the rest of the family were in the den watching a delayed broadcast of an interview I gave on the subject of sex. When the program was over, she turned to me and said, "Doris, you really look better in person than you do on TV." And that was as far as the discussion went.

I am grateful to Elizabeth Deichman for suggesting to Prometheus Books that I write this book, and to Steven L. Mitchell, my editor, for his special help, and to Dr. Marilyn Bell for her encouragement. I am indebted to Camilla Monin and to Irene Walsh for their assistance, and to Sister Jackie Weigle for keeping me on track and finding everything I needed. She, as well as some very special friends over the years, epitomizes the love that is at the very basis of our sexuality. And while speaking of love, an enormous amount goes to Dawn Hewitt, who has handled the word processing for this book so carefully, just as she used to take care of this absent-minded professor for so many years.

I feel that I have journeyed through this book with my husband, Ted, at my side, where he has been now for thirty-four years. The journey has been fun. I hope you, the reader, will enjoy your journey as well.

Doris Hammond, Ph.D. 1987

Contents

1

Myths and Facts of Sexual Aging

What I Always Thought But Never Knew

"There are many females who never feel any sexual excitement whatever; others, again, to a limited degree, are capable of experiencing it. The best mothers, wives and managers of households know little or nothing of the sexual pleasure. Love of homes, children and domestic duties are the only passions they feel. As a rule, the modest woman submits to her husband, but only to please him; and, but for the desire of maternity, would far rather be relieved from his attentions. This is doubly true of women during the periods when they are with child, and when they are nursing."

Eugenics, 1915

Each individual is allotted just so many sexual experiences and when they are all used up, that's the end of sexual activity for that person.

Let us assume that everyone knows this to be a myth, but it is because our sexuality has been so misunderstood and surrounded by ignorance that such a ridiculous notion has been accepted. Myths concerning sexuality have persisted throughout the history of Western culture. Of these many myths, perhaps the most difficult to dispel concern the sexual ability, activity, and interest of older persons. Our older citizens are often caught in the turmoil that these myths cause. The professionals or service providers who work with elders, and each family member who loves them, must first have an understanding of his or her own sexuality and possess an openness to the sexuality of others in order to help dispel these myths. Yet, it is this discussion of our own sexuality that can cause the most embarrassment and, when coupled with lack of correct information, perpetuates some very interesting myths. It can cause a person whose job it is to provide support for elderly persons, and a family member whose desire it is to reinforce the life satisfaction of a parent or grandparent, to be totally ineffective in dealing with what may be a major or underlying cause of the older person's depression or negative adjustment to aging.

One thing that almost all of us worry about is whether what we do or think within a sexual context is "normal." If we think about it, we realize that the sexual activity in which we engage tends to develop and change with time. What we considered "normal" as twenty-year-olds may change and expand by the time we are forty or sixty or eighty. But what standards do we apply when we decide whether something is normal? Mostly, we don't bother to think rationally before applying a standard. Instead, we tend to have an immediate, gut-level, emotional reaction based upon what we have learned from our parents and from society. For instance, test yourself on this:

You are walking through a park during the daylight hours, when you come upon two persons sitting on a park bench. They are kissing and hugging, totally immersed in each other and completely oblivious to anyone or anything around them. Upon looking closer, you find they are

(1) a young man and a young woman—

What is your reaction: (check) _____ good for them, _____ okay, _____ sweet, _____ undignified, _____ shameful, _____ perverse, _____ should be arrested;

(2) an old man and an old woman—

What is your reaction: (check) _____ good for them, _____ okay, _____ sweet, _____ undignified, _____ shameful, _____ perverse, _____ should be arrested;

(3) an old man and a young woman—

What is your reaction: (check) _____ good for them, _____ okay, _____ sweet, _____ undignified, _____ shameful, _____ perverse, _____ should be arrested;

(4) an old woman and a young man—

What is your reaction: (check) _____ good for them, _____ okay, _____ sweet, _____ undignified, _____ shameful, _____ perverse, _____ should be arrested;

(5) two women—

What is your reaction: (check) _____ good for them, _____ okay, _____ sweet, _____ undignified, _____ shameful, _____ perverse, _____ should be arrested;

(6) two men—

What is your reaction: (check) _____ good for them, _____ okay, _____ sweet, _____ undignified, _____ shameful, _____ perverse, _____ should be arrested.

Were you honest with your answers? Did you really visualize the situation and not just intellectualize it? If you did, chances are you found differences in your reactions. Why?

Now, ask yourself these questions:

(1) Did I tell anyone about what I saw?
(2) How many times did I repeat the story?

Most people would probably not bother even mentioning having seen the young man and the young woman on the park bench. The other couple combinations would probably be reported to at least one other person, some to more than one. In fact, the incident might become a favorite "story to tell" that might even be repeated for years to come. Again, I ask, "Why?" Why do some behaviors seem normal to us and others are not? I am nearsighted so I take my glasses *off* in order to read. That's not really normal, but no one calls it deviant. It has to do with my optic equipment, not my sexuality, so it's okay.

We can define normalcy from several perspectives. From a statistical (numerical) perspective we might point out that approximately 90 percent of our population is heterosexual and 10 percent is homosexual. From a biological perspective we might ask what it is that other mammals do. From a moral perspective we might look at what religion teaches us. Legal perspectives let us know what the law allows. Finally, a sociological perspective asks us to consider what is in the best interests of society. Which perspective or combination of perspectives are to be used when deciding what is normal?

Do you examine your own sexuality, or are you too busy examining the sexuality of others? Perhaps you choose to ignore the whole shameful topic altogether. If you examine your own sexuality, as you should, along with the sexuality of others, you will find no easy answers forthcoming. Perhaps the only standard that seems comfortable to apply is that of tolerance. We not only cause others, such as the elderly, to suffer psychologically and emotionally as a result of our lack of tolerance, but we cause ourselves considerable psychological and emotional harm as well. We suffer from thinking that we are using our bodies "abnormally" if, for example, we engage in oral sex or masturbate, or that we are using our minds in strange ways if we entertain sexual fantasies.

If we were more tolerant of ourselves, of our humanness, we would be making the necessary first step in being tolerant of others, such as the older couple on the park bench. What we now think to be inappropriate behavior for older people, we will consider inappropriate behavior for ourselves when we are older. This becomes a self-fulfilling prophecy that goes on through the generations. A homosexual physician once wrote that sexuality is basically neither right nor wrong, good nor bad, only variable.

Much of what has been taught to us as right or wrong, good or bad behavior has been influenced and reinforced by myths heard so often that they become confused with fact. Sexuality confuses us; we are taught so little about it that myths spring up in abundance thereby helping us to obscure the truth.

Before we look at sexual myths, especially those relating to the elderly, a discussion of myths in general might allow us to better understand their enormous influence. Myths are created to explain what we don't understand, and they flourish because they help to act as shields, protecting us from the knowledge we are afraid to know. As such, they give us comfort, something to "hang our hat on." We even quote these myths to others, no matter how implausible they may be. They guard us from anxiety and insecurity and keep us from thinking deeply about something. As improbable as a myth may sound to our intellect, it appeals to our emotions.

It would be a mistake to assume that myths are held only by the uneducated and the less intelligent. Highly educated people hold a number of curious sexual misconceptions. To demonstrate this, I often ask students which child learns to be prejudiced faster, given the same teaching and role modeling, the brighter or the duller child. Almost without exception the students will answer that it is the duller child. Gleefully, which is always my manner when I can catch them on something, I answer, "No, the brighter. Can you figure out why?" It may take a while for the answer, but finally a student will arrive at the realization that a brighter child learns everything faster, fact or fiction. A corollary, of course, is that the brighter child can also unlearn prejudice faster. So, too, with myths. Those we learn but never re-examine become part of us. I hope this book will help to dispel some of the myths we have learned, especially those that deal with sexuality in general and older persons' sexuality in particular.

Regardless of age, level of education, or socioeconomic status, certain myths may still be held that somehow have been filtered through to us as fact. Perhaps the greatest hope that myths will be identified for what they are is our improved modern communications. Our society has become significantly more informed about sexual matters. Media "sexperts" such as Dr. Ruth Westheimer, spur us on to consider previously unquestioned sexual mythology.

Let's examine some myths that our parents and grandparents grew up with. Did you believe some of these myths, too? Do you *still* believe some of them? Do your parents; your grandparents? Why not ask your parents and grandparents about them? It could be the start of a fascinating conversation and the beginning of a willingness to talk to one another about sexual matters, I have had great fun sharing myths with audiences and they are always able to provide me with some additional ones that I had never heard before. Here are just a few of the many myths that abound.

MYTHS

1. Women should not shower, take a bath, or wash their hair during menstruation; nor should they engage in sports.
2. A girl is not a virgin if her hymen (membrane covering entrance to the vagina) has been broken.
3. Sexual intercourse before any athletic competition reduces the excellence of athletic performance.
4. Impotence in older men is always the result of physical factors.
5. A large penis is of great importance to a woman's sexual gratification.
6. Vaginal orgasm, rather than clitoral, is the only "real" kind of orgasm.
7. Sexual intercourse should be avoided during menstruation and during pregnancy.
8. Each person is allotted only so many sexual experiences; when they are used up, sexual activity ends.
9. Sterilization of a man or a woman reduces sex drive.
10. A woman's sex life is terminated by the onset of menopause or after a hysterectomy has been performed.
11. Tall, muscular men have the largest penises.
12. There is an absolutely "safe" period for sexual intercourse when a woman cannot become pregnant.
13. Vasectomy is 100 percent effective as a birth control measure.
14. Alcohol is a sexual stimulant.
15. An unborn child can be "marked." For instance if a pregnant woman is frightened by a rat, a birthmark in the shape of a rat might appear on the baby. If the mother eats too many strawberries, a mark in the shape of a strawberry appears.
16. People are either totally homosexual or totally heterosexual.

17. Childhood exposure to a homosexual adult is an important factor in a young person later becoming a homosexual.
18. Homosexuals are identifiable by their appearance.
19. Frequent masturbation causes insanity.
20. Masturbation causes many physical manifestations, such as warts, hair in the palms of the hands, pimples, and impotence.
21. Masturbation is a practice restricted almost exclusively to men.
22. Any person infected with gonorrhea will develop symptoms within a week after sexual contact.
23. Vaginal-penile intercourse is the only "normal" method of having sexual relations.
24. Rapists and other sex offenders are oversexed.
25. Married couples may legally engage in any sexual activity they mutually agree upon.
26. Physicians are generally well trained in sexual problems and are willing to deal with their patients' emotional needs.
27. Douching (cleansing of the uterine area) is a particularly effective birth control method.
28. Young adults of today are "going wild" sexually.
29. Sex education has no place in our schools because (choose favorite myth): it is a Communist plot to destroy our country from within; it leads to sexual acting-out behavior; it causes a rise in promiscuity; it increases premarital pregnancy, ...
30. Acquired Immune Deficiency Syndrome (AIDS) is a punishment from God for homosexual behavior.

The above constitute a sample of the hundreds of myths weighing heavy on the minds of old and young alike. Did you know that they were all myths? Do you know what the facts actually are? Let's imagine the opportunity really has arisen to speak with parents or grandparents about some of these. Or maybe you, as a parent or grandparent, need to be the one to introduce the subject. After all, your children and/or grandchildren couldn't possibly imagine that you might be interested in sex, so it may be up to you to address the subject.

What are the facts that can challenge these myths?

FACTS

1. There is no problem caused by getting wet when menstruating. Prior to the advent of tampons, it may have been inconvenient to go swimming, but nothing else. Likewise, sports of any kind are fine and only to be limited if the woman just doesn't feel up to it as a result of menstrual cramping. One woman's group I spoke to added several corollary myths: Never touch your plants because they will die; don't bake because the cake won't rise; don't have a permanent because it won't "take."

2. The hymen can be broken in ways unrelated to sexual intercourse. The young woman is usually never aware that it has broken. In some societies, an intact hymen has been a prerequisite to marriage; in some cases it was considered so important that a fake hymen was manufactured and inserted to replace the broken one.

3. Limiting sexual activity the night before athletic competition always seemed to me to be a justification coaches used in order to get all their players in and accounted for on time.

4. Psychological factors can play an important role in the impotence of men, both old and young. Psychologically induced impotence is treatable and, therefore, reversible. It is easy to check for psychological impotence. If an erection occurs during a man's sleep, it is a psychological rather than a physiological problem.

5. A woman's vaginal barrel expands to fit the size of the particular penis inserted; therefore, whatever the size, there is no difference in feeling, unless she is psychologically "turned on" by the sight of a large penis. Additionally, the stimulation of the clitoris is what causes the most satisfaction, not the stimulation of the vaginal walls.

6. It is unfortunate that Sigmund Freud led us to believe that a vaginal orgasm must be the goal. I wonder how many women in the past (and the present, too) have not experienced the joy of an orgasm due to his pronouncement. An orgasm is an orgasm is an orgasm.

7. Sexual intercourse should be avoided only a few weeks before delivery. Otherwise, there is no medical reason not to enjoy sexual activity. Sexual intercourse during menstruation, and the lack thereof, is more a religious taboo brought about by biblical teachings.[1]

8. I am not sure where the myth of using up your sexual experiences began, but I do know that on one South Sea island, each time a man ejaculated, he put a notch on a stick; when the notches accumulated to a preordained number, he was all finished because the ejaculate was used up. Apparently no one ever tried ejaculating beyond the designated number of times, as this never was disproven. Or perhaps they did and the psychological impact of this magic number was so strong that it affected the physical possibility.

9. There is no correlation whatsoever between sterilization and sex drive, unless your *mind* tells you there is.

10. Neither menopause nor a hysterectomy is a cause for reduced sexual desire in women. Older people who may still feel that sex is only for procreation might stop indulging for that reason alone. Others find that this time of their lives provides added sexual enjoyment. (This will be discussed in a later chapter.)

11. There is little difference in the size of penises when in full erection, even when there is considerable difference at the flaccid stage.

12. Those who may have thought there is an absolutely "safe" period for sexual intercourse have probably won awards at local Mother's Day celebrations for "most children."

13. Those who may have thought that vasectomy is 100 percent effective may not win the aforementioned award, but it's possible that they are sending a child through college. Admittedly, though not 100 percent effective (is anything?), vasectomy is an excellent means of birth control.

14. Alcohol is *not* a sexual stimulant, contrary to popular thinking. It may enhance the ability to lose inhibitions but, once lost, the influence of alcohol lessens one's ability to do anything about it.

15. The birthmark myth is still alive and well, *and* false. If each of us were to contribute a birthmark story to a central file in my office, I would have enough material for another book.

16. Professionals in the area of human sexuality agree that homosexuality-heterosexuality, rather than an either-or circumstance, is really on a continuum, somewhat like a natural curve. These professionals generally agree with Carl Jung's description of the masculine and feminine in all of us. (More about this later in the chapter on homosexuality.)

17. Studies have shown that a child growing up in a home with homosexual parents has no greater proclivity for homosexuality than a child growing up in a heterosexual home. Exposure to homosexual teachers, friends, workmates, likewise has no effect.

18. If you believe the appearance myth, you may be confusing homosexuals with transvestites, who are not homosexuals at all. Transvestites dress like women (or men), but rarely exhibit homosexual behavior. Some of the most masculine men are gay and some of the most feminine women are lesbian. The limp wristed males and butch females are stereotypical and few in number.

19. Do you know where the masturbation-lunacy myth began? In the old insane asylums. Patients were observed masturbating in far greater numbers when confined than was the case in the normal population. The assumption was that they went crazy because they masturbated. I wonder how many years went by before it occurred to anyone that patients were masturbating *because* they were in an institution. They didn't have a partner in order to do the one thing that still felt good to them, given the circumstances of their situation.

20. Aren't the physical manifestations of masturbation an awesome list? Add to this list early decrepitude, nervous afflictions, blindness, loss of memory, hemorrhaging, falling of the womb, cancer, cardiac disorders, palpitations, hysteria, convulsions, and emaciation. No

wonder the old textbooks never use the word "masturbation" but instead refer to it as "self-abuse." Also, no wonder masturbation is a problem for many of our older people who have been exposed to this horrible information.

21. Masturbation is certainly a popular practice among men (over 90 percent) but it is not exclusive to this sex. Over 80 percent of women have also masturbated at one time or another.

22. Gonorrhea is an insidious disease. An individual can be infected, without symptoms, yet remain contagious for a long time. Another myth, shared with me recently during a speaking engagement, is that gonorrhea happens to blacks whereas syphillis happens to whites.

23. Vaginal-penile intercourse being the only "normal" method for sexual relations refers us back to our discussion of what is "normal."

24. Sex offenders, such as rapists, are not oversexed. Actually, this offense has to do with aggression and power, and not with sex.

25. Couples may *think* they can engage in any type of sexual activity they mutually agree upon, but they will find that in many states what they are doing is illegal. For instance, the state of Georgia identifies any sexual activity as illegal except that between a man and a woman in the male-dominant position. Usually couples can feel protected in the privacy of their own bedroom, but even that is in question due to the recent arrest of a consenting homosexual couple *in* the "privacy" of their own bedroom.

26. Unfortunately many physicians are unable and/or unwilling to deal with their patients' sexual concerns. If you or any member of your family is seeking a physician, find one who can and will accept your sexual problems as important. As human beings we are also sexual beings; thus there are problems related to sexuality that could affect other parts of our total being, just as the many problems we encounter in life could affect our sexuality. A doctor must be able to treat us as total human (sexual) beings. For instance, be aware that the depression you notice in an older family member could be caused by an unresolved and unspoken sexual issue. Your doctor *must* be aware of this.

27. Douching, rather than being an effective birth control method, has been known to push the sperm farther up into the vagina, thereby making impregnation *more* likely. I might add that douching, so long thought to be hygenically necessary, is now suggested only under direction from a physician and for a specific reason. The natural fluids of a woman's body are enough to provide the necessary cleansing.

28. Even before the AIDS scare, the young people of today were not as wild as everyone seemed to think. There may have been a lot of talk about sex but results of surveys taken on adolescent sexual behavior are often sensationalized by the media and their methodologies are often questioned.[2]

29. Many studies have shown that sex education does not increase the incidence of sexual intercourse and unwanted pregnancy. The myth persists, however, as the minds of some remain closed to the facts.

30. AIDS as a punishment from God is the most recent and perhaps most illogical and frightening myth. Even if we see God as a punishing Being, would he also punish those people who are suffering and have died from AIDS because they received a needed blood transfusion? Would he punish little children with AIDS? Nevertheless, the myth persists. A minister suggested that if we believe this myth, then God must really hate gays but love lesbians, since the latter are the least at risk.

Talk about these myths with your friends and family. It's one way to start communicating about sex in general. Then, for the sake of your older friends and family members, and ultimately for your own benefit, consider the following five myths that are specific to older adults:[3]

MYTHS

1. Older people do not have sexual desires.

2. Older people couldn't make love even if they wanted to.

3. Older people are so physically fragile that sex might hurt them.

4. Older people are physically unattractive and, therefore, sexually undesirable.
5. The whole notion of sex for older people is shameful and decidedly perverse.

Would an older person in your family agree with these myths? Do *you* agree with these myths? Let's look at the facts.

FACTS

1. Older people *do* have sexual desires. We are sexual beings from birth to death. Although there may be decreases in levels of arousal and a lessening in intensity, along with a slowing down of response, older people desire the closeness and touching that is so much a part of our humanness. Yes, grandmas and grandpas still desire each other much as they always have.
2. Why do we think older people couldn't make love even if they wanted to? Do we think they can't still bake a cake? Swim? Read a book? Fix a car? Why can't they make love? Have they forgotten how? Or, perhaps, it is the judgment of society that they can't anymore and probably don't want to anyway. First of all, we know that they *can* and *do* make love. Sexual activity drops off in the sixties for women and in the seventies for men, but for many—especially those who have partners—there is little decrease. One wonders how much the self-fulfilling prophecy of the older years as sexless years has caused this decrease. When these folks were younger, they probably felt that people become "neutered" with age, so in their own old age they perpetuate the myth.
3. Older people are too fragile and sex might hurt them. On the contrary, sex helps older people both physically and psychologically. Only the very frail and those in extreme poor health seem to be nonresponsive. Sex can actually be therapeutic. It can relieve the pain of arthritis as it increases the output of cortisone. (For continued relief, however, it has been suggested that one would have to have sex every four hours!) Likewise, it is a great pain reliever for

backaches. The older person who is sexually active needs fewer tranquilizers and antidepressants. Having sex has even been thought to add to longevity, while encouraging a stronger sense of self. The psychological benefits of maintaining a sense of self have been documented throughout our life span.

Some people have the mistaken notion that sex can cause death, especially in older people. No greater percentage of deaths occur during intercourse than during any other activity that expends the same amount of energy. Even when intercourse is with a "secret" partner, the added stress this brings about causes little rise in the incidence of death. Perhaps the best advice is to keep in practice with sex, just as you keep in practice with tennis or any other activity.

4. Society (and we're part of it!) has really done a job on us with respect to viewing older people as physically unattractive and, therefore, sexually undesirable. This myth contains within it another myth: that only physically attractive people want to have sex with each other. There are a lot of physically unattractive (by society's standards) younger people who would disagree. Maybe someone who is attractive to you is not attractive to me; I may not want to have sex with him, but you might! That's what keeps all of us from wanting to have sex with the same person. Thank goodness for that! But to lump all older people into the category of being unattractive just because they are old is an insult. I might add that this myth is particularly hard on the older woman, for she is the one more often judged as physically unattractive, whereas the older man is often considered still attractive, or distinguished at the very least.
5. Many older people feel that sexual thoughts of any kind are shameful, if not perverse. The roots of this will be explored in the next chapter. But many are beginning to believe otherwise, and their ranks are growing. It is children who have the hardest time accepting the sexuality of their parents and grandparents. In fact, a child's view of his or her parents' sexuality often takes a tougher line than the parents' view of their children's and adolescents' sexuality. This, too, will be explored in depth in a future chapter and is a major emphasis of this book. I will focus on the need to become comfort-

able with parents and grandparents as sexual beings, the need for parents and grandparents to become comfortable with themselves as sexual beings, and the need to identify and understand our own sexuality.

As a counter to the myth that older people are sexless or uninterested in sex, we have to be careful not to accept an opposing myth, which claims that older people are *as* interested in sex now as when they were young. The traditional norms were an escape from sex, but contemporary norms are a reflection of our culture's frantic search for the fountain of youth. Also, we must be careful not to impose sex upon those for whom it is not held up as a top priority. Continuity of life is what we must strive for.

Normative expectations must be developed that separate youthful sex and aging sex without implying that one is a degenerative form of the other. Aging sex is quantitatively different from youthful sex and is to be enjoyed in and of itself. Older people too often become the objects of jokes and are frequently ridiculed as "dirty old men" or "senile old women." Popular opinion has them steadily declining into oblivion. Even though the sexuality of older people is not identical to that of the young, their need for intimacy and sexual expression endures.

NOTES

1. The Holy Bible, Leviticus 15: 19–24.
2. William H. Masters, Virginia E. Johnson, and Robert C. Kolodry, *Human Sexuality* (Boston: Little, Brown and Co., 1982), 194–95.
3. Robert N. Butler and Myra I. Lewis, *Aging and Mental Health* (St. Louis, Mo.: C. V. Mosby Co., 1977), 112.

2

Cultural, Religious, and Societal Influences

Breaking Away from Tradition

"It seems to be the sentiment, all but universal, that the husband should be the older, say from five to ten years.

One writer says: 'I think there should always be an interval of about ten years between a man of mature age and his wife. Women age much more rapidly than do men, and as the peculiar functions of matrimony should cease in both parties about the same time, such interval as this is evidently desirable.'"

Eugenics, 1915

An old couple were reminiscing about how they used to make love. The woman said, "Oh, Frank, remember how you used to kiss me and nibble my ear. I wish you'd do that again." "Okay," said Frank, "hand me my teeth."

Our values concerning how we think about sex and how we conduct ourselves as sexual beings are acquired in much the same way as we acquire values that guide us in other areas of social life. They are acquired through the "ultimate authority" of sacred scripture, from education, from folk wisdom found in legends and old wives tales, through common conversation, from jokes and cliché phrases, and from the media. From these authorities we adopt major assumptions about what is good and bad sexually, what is appropriate and inappropriate, and what incites pleasure or induces repugnance. These clusters of assumptions operate as sexual value systems and are internalized by our personality structure. Most of our values become set in place at or about the age of ten; they then change slowly, usually with great effort or at the prompting of a significant emotional event. It is important, therefore, that we recognize the influences that surrounded our older population when they were very young, from around the turn of the century to the 1930s.

Religion has been, and continues to be, a strong influence on our sexual expression. In the Judeo-Christian tradition of Western societies, the Old and New Testament prohibitions against sexuality in both its specific and general forms have proven to be an immensely powerful force. They have demanded and justified repression of sexual thought and conduct; provided heavy burdens of guilt and shame; and have even suggested that expressing sexuality is a sign of satanic lure. Explicit prohibitions can be found against nakedness, intercourse during the menstrual period, extramarital sex, masturbation, and homosexuality. St. Paul's first letter to the Corinthians contains an outright condemnation of intercourse. There are less explicitly sexual, but clearly sexist viewpoints that depict women as tricking honorable men into degradation. Women are portrayed as sorrow-laden helpers of the dominant male, and are even presumed to have evil powers.[1] It is easy to see how a woman's self-image can suffer in such a repressive environment.

In contrast to these Judeo-Christian prohibitions are the joyful, yet spiritual Hindu "verses of desire" found in the *Kama Sutra*. This religiously-oriented philosophy advocates a balance between spiritual, material, cultural, and sensual realms of life. It even gives elaborate instruction regarding activities and techniques that can be used in attaining the highest possible realms of sensual and sexual pleasure. In the Chinese philosophy of Confucius, and later in Taoist persuasions, sexual climax is viewed as a transcendence of earthly existence. Sexual technique is discussed in a manner that can only be described as beautiful. The orientation of different cultures toward sexuality is even revealed in the very language used. For instance, the Yellow Emperor of China referred to sexual intercourse as "the Clouds and the Rain," and to female orgasm as "Fire in the Jade Temple." In contrast, St. Augustine thought of sensual desire (what he called "concupiscence") as a key element in the inherent corruption of man and as the sinful product of carnal lust.[2]

Perhaps the most sexually impoverished culture found anywhere is a group of remote Irish villagers, living on an island off the mainland. These extremely religious villagers possess a strong body taboo and thus very little transfer of sexual information takes place among them. There is such a dearth of information that "old wives' tales" do not exist to be passed on. Babies are kept fully clothed no matter how hot the weather, and sexual intercourse is conducted between those who can overcome the obstacle of multiple layers of clothing. In this fishing village the men cover up completely even when at sea. One can easily imagine the effects on the sexuality of these people compared to the nonrestrictive society that exists in some South Sea island communities.

Such repressive influences are important for understanding the sexual attitudes of some of our parents and grandparents, who came to this country from a different culture and upon whom very specific values were inculcated. While in the United States they were raised in a home environment that strongly reflected the expectations of the "old country." Also, contrasts such as these help to explain why the elderly, as with any other age group, are quite unique from each other. In fact, it is probable that the various elderly groups are more different from each other than members of any other age group, for they have had longer to become diversified.

Political structures can also strongly influence sexual conduct. In South Africa, a society saturated with racial fear and hatred, there are laws forbidding sexual conduct between members of the presumed "superior race" and those belonging to the culturally-defined "inferior race." Nazi Germany also had such laws. It was not so long ago that the United States had laws against interracial marriage or sexual relations (what was called "miscegenation") of whites with other races. Again, these effects are felt by those who had their values imposed upon them. Our own Pentagon insists that it is not making a moral judgment in its revised rules on what sort of sex acts disqualify personnel from obtaining security clearances, but critics say the broad new action "looks like a witch hunt." The new regulation includes adultery and sodomy in its definition of "sexual misconduct." Conduct that could disqualify someone from holding a security clearance includes acts performed with a minor or with animals, child molestation, incest, prostitution, pandering, sexual harassment, and self-mutilation. It also covers "adultery that is recent, frequent, and likely to continue"; transsexualism; transvestism; exhibitionism; voyeurism; spouse-swapping; sodomy; or group sex orgies. It is said to be needed because previous guidelines were vague and misleading in their effort to weed out individuals who might be susceptible to blackmail by enemy spies. Any effort to target homosexuals was denied, but critics contend that the new rule has cast doubt on the fairness of the Pentagon's treatment of homosexuality. They feel that there are few people who could not be disqualified under the new regulation.

Certainly our feelings of male superiority are rooted in the thousands of years that have witnessed most cultures placing males in positions of dominance, power, control, and even ownership of females. This is obvious in the biblical reference to Adam and Eve and in both Indian and Chinese sexual philosophies. It is also found in explicit sexual discussions, assumptions, and jokes. The man always has the greater sex drive. One joke has a psychologist talking with a shriveled-up, old man puffing an enormous cigar. The psychologist asks, "How many cigars do you smoke a day?" "About twenty!" the old man replies. "Well, that must substitute for other things, like drinking?" "No siree. I drink a quart of whiskey every day." "How about women?" "Women?! I've got two call girls out-of-town, my wife, and a secretary at home!" The psychologist, obviously impressed, asks, "Do you mind if I ask your age?" "Of course not. I'm twenty-five." Our older population grew up assuming that the man has a stronger sex drive, initiates and then controls the action with the male-on-top or "missionary" position, and terminates the action since male orgasm is the primary objective of intercourse.

Each culture defines for itself certain body characteristics or personality and interactive patterns that are thought to be most attractive. The Western concept of romantic love fits with the concept of male dominance in that the woman is expected to make herself "attractive" and then wait patiently to be swept off her feet by some man. We all know this is changing but it was what the older generation believed to be the only appropriate way to behave, and many feel it still is the most appropriate.

Our culture idealizes romantic love (our institutionalized form of relationship) that will lead to marriage. Our business relationships are formed outside of marriage. The custom, however, among the Turu people in East Africa involves a pattern in which the husband and wife marry for the purpose of forming a business partnership and are free to form romantic relationships outside the marriage. This allows for both business and romance to flourish without one being a problem to the other in either culture, but how differently the end result is arrived at.[3] In India it is common for marriages to be arranged by parents. Interestingly, not only are divorces practically unheard of there, but the measured levels of satisfaction of the married partners is much higher than our own.

American sexual values are strongly influenced by the "work ethic." That might seem like a strange statement, but not if we look at it in the context of evaluated performance and anxiety over possible "failure." Also, isn't orgasm seen as the product of love-making, and the "work" of sex to produce a child (procreation)? However, it can be argued that more recently in America sex is involving play (recreation). What reason for having sex did our seniors learn?

It may be argued that human sexuality is basically the same everywhere; however, every society controls the expression of sexuality in some manner. Particular behaviors vary from group to group and there are large cross-cultural variations that exist in patterns of actual sexual behavior. It must be remembered that each elderly person may have a different cultural influence affecting him or her, perhaps even more so than cultural influences affect individuals in other age groups where greater mobility and fewer ties to the "home" country are common. Professionals and laypeople who work with the elderly, and close family members, need to be aware of the cultural, religious, and societal forces affecting their own value systems in order to better understand and respond to these cultural forces affecting the value systems of elders.

Sexual decline that may occur in an older person is more an artifact of social prohibitions and partner availability than it is a biological factor. Although there are some cultural restrictions on the older male, his sexuality is primarily limited by physical capacity. Conversely, the older female is limited more by cultural factors rather than physical ones since aging does not substantially affect the sexual capacity of females, compared to males. The double standard remains alive and well as a cultural factor that can impede sexual fulfillment. There are many more widows than widowers. Women average more than a decade of widowhood because they will live more than seven years longer than their male counterparts and will have married someone approximately three years older than themselves. Biology plays cruel tricks on females, leaving a large army of women without partners. One trick that society plays is making it seem the "rule" that men should be older than the women they marry and then, in old age, making it all right for the few remaining elder men to marry young women while deeming it inappropriate for older women to marry or have any sort of relationship with younger men. (See the Appendix for Benjamin Franklin's eight reasons to marry an older woman.)

Various solutions have been proposed. An obvious one is for a woman to marry a younger man. An added benefit of this suggestion would be that the two would be sexually more in tune, since a man reaches his sexual peak at age eighteen and a woman at age thirty (not a biological difference, but rather because it takes her longer to uncover the sexual self that society for so many years has determined she should repress). How about polygamy for women as a possible solution? Would homosexual relationships among women who did not previously exhibit that identity be a solution that society could support? Can we as a society recognize the need for human contact, caring, and touching as one that transcends any age or gender confinement? Society needs to take a closer look at age discrepant relationships and alternative life styles, not as indicating psychopathology but rather as a mentally healthy way to choose mates based upon psychological compatibility rather than social standards of propriety and normalcy. How we address ourselves to these and other issues will have a great deal to do with how we grow as a society and how we express our own sexuality.

The social world in which today's elderly grew up would not have allowed them to examine what I have suggested in the previous paragraph. Even the most "liberated" knew little of the "facts of life," and most held to strong superstitions and to a puritan ethic. They were greatly affected by the Victorian era. It certainly wasn't a healthy climate for exploring sexual problems. In fact, it was totally inappropriate for examining problems of any sort through open communication. Everything was to be left within the family. Never "wash your linen in public" was the creed of the day. With the family failing to communicate about sexual problems, they remained hidden. Family members still have difficulty talking about sex with each other, which is the real reason for this book. Sex remains a mystery. No wonder those who lived during previous eras are often shocked when presented with ways of solving the mystery of sex, since sexual discussions had never really been a part of the family pow-wows.

Our society is careful to admonish older people to "act your age." This becomes a very real problem for older people who are not sure what this means. Whether actually heard from a family member or assumed through the conditioning of an age conscious society, perhaps the only safe way to behave is to sit in a rocking chair. At least we know what we are permitted to do, even if society sometimes thinks we are so old we can't even get it (the rocking chair) going. Each one of us has had moments when we are sure someone is wishing we would "act our age." When young we shouldn't act too old, when older we shouldn't act too young. How about the two old people on the park bench holding hands and kissing? In the first place, the admonition to "act your age" would probably prevent them from even being on the bench in the first place. Just one curious look from anyone passing by and they would be sure to assume that the person is thinking, "Act your age!" and they would probably be right. What would they do then? Probably leave hurriedly, maybe even in separate directions, or, at the very least, move to opposite sides of the bench and be satisfied with sharing a secretive glance now and then. Even if we give the benefit of the doubt to the passerby as someone who is supportive of, or at least open-minded toward their behavior, that enlightened passerby will still probably describe what he or she sees as "cute." How often we relegate the behavior of older people to that of children by describing it as cute: "Don't they look cute?" "Aren't they sweet?" We rarely describe their behavior, or their appearance, in adult terms, and we certainly don't do so when it comes to their sexual behavior or appearance. Upon hearing that an elder man made a sexually suggestive remark, we think him either senile or a dirty old man. That same remark, made by a younger man, however, would be considered "macho." When we see an older woman dressed attractively and in good health and physical condition, we say she "looks young for her age." That *is* her age and that's how she looks *at* that age, not as a younger caricature of her age.

How often do we change the tone of our voice when we talk to older people? It's as though they have become children. This is the "kindergarten voice," the voice so often affected by kindergarten teachers when they talk to their children. Have you ever found yourself talking in a higher pitch and using simpler terms, as though the older person couldn't understand? What an insult! The logical end to this type of thinking is that we view elders as childish beings, playing house with each other, rather than as mature individuals expressing a sexual maturity gained through years of loving.

We live in an age of "isms." First we learned about racism and then about sexism. To this has been added another, *ageism*. As examples of prejudiced viewpoints—racism toward people of a different race, sexism toward people of a different sex—and as awful as each is in its particulars, I would like to suggest that ageism is perhaps the most difficult of all to understand. Why? If we are racist, we will never be of another race; if we are sexist, we will never (with rare exceptions) be another sex. However, if we are ageist, we will, in the end (barring premature death), be the beneficiaries of our own ridiculous prejudice. Think about that the next time you make judgments based upon age. Remember what the only alternative to aging is. . . .

Have you noticed how all old people are thought of as the same—old? Nothing else, just old. That includes the notion that all old people don't enjoy sex. Some don't, but some young people don't either. A mistake is made when stratifying people into groups by age and then identifying each individual as having all the characteristics we assign to his or her particular group.

In our society, where beauty and youth reign supreme, I am not surprised to hear a student wonder how someone could be sexually turned on by a partner who is gray and wrinkly. This student offered the opinion that *he* certainly couldn't be attracted to such a person. Maybe the comment of an older couple, married forty-five years, makes it clear that a sexual turn-on doesn't occur just because of outer beauty but because "forty-five years of loving each other is a turn-on in itself." Most younger people wouldn't think about that.

Only recently have television advertisements begun to picture older people with any sense of vitality or health. Even now there are still some pretty depressing and ridiculous older people being featured. A recent advertisement showed a married couple with the husband in obvious need of support from his wife for everyday living. The product being sold was one that could be helpful in that kind of situation. I am sure the company's marketing staff provided the correct information, that in most cases it would be the wife as caregiver, but why picture her husband as some whimpering, simpering, pathetic nonbeing; and her as this oversolicitous, mechanical wife?

Television, magazine covers, and movies continue to have a difficult time portraying older people as anything but sexless, doting caricatures. Television has a tremendous impact on our children, but how many of them watch "The Golden Girls," the first attempt to portray older women as sexual and exciting? Have they watched "The Phil Donohue Show" to learn, through his segments dealing with sexuality and older persons, that grandmas and grandpas really are interested? Recently, I was disappointed in a portrayal of an older teacher on "Bronx Zoo," a new television series. Today's programming should not perpetuate the image of poor little old ladies who can't hack it, especially since this show is about a high school, which would attract a potentially large audience of school-age viewers. In this segment, the teachers had to pass a test given by the state. The writers made sure the black teachers passed, even making it clear their scores were higher than most of the white teachers, so that stereotype was taken care of. But guess who didn't pass? The sweet little old lady. The writers depicted her as taking this failure very well, by having her sweetly state that she just couldn't keep up with the times and all the changes. An older teacher, whose mind is constantly being challenged, would not lose his or her ability to do well on that test. But now, after watching that show, children *know* that getting old must mean becoming too dumb to pass a test and, having done so, accepting failure as a natural course of events.

Magazine covers continue to present their audiences with nubile young girls who look out at us in various stages of dress and undress, taunting us with a look that is oh so sexy but who couldn't actually know what real sex is all about. They just haven't lived long enough. It's about time we see the middle-aged and older men and women looking at us with the wisdom of experience in their eyes, being portrayed as sexual beings. The more covers of this nature, the more television shows like "The Golden Girls," the more sensitized society will become to the worth of its older citizens.

For years movies have used older actors and actresses in character roles only. Men, however, have always fared better. The list of names is endless of men who, in their "mature years," were still considered great lovers. Don't most women still adore Paul Newman? But what of older women? Either the well-known names have disappeared from the screen, as though they no longer existed, or these actresses were saddled with sexless, often demented, roles. There are too many "Baby Janes"!

Society puts the onus of beauty on women. Women grew up thinking they were desirable only if they were cheerleaders or beauty contest winners. It is not difficult to imagine what this does to women as they get older. No woman who is old is truly considered beautiful. Many famous female stars have had total "make overs" to continue looking young. Young women who identify themselves as having self-worth only because of their beauty find that self-worth diminished in middle and old age. These are the women who, when seeing the first signs of aging, lose their sense of self and are prime candidates for severe depression and other adjustment problems. Some of the best advice students can receive is to be grateful they were not raving beauties while growing up. Without the element of beauty influencing their decisions, they were more likely to develop another part of themselves that would make them feel special throughout life. The beautiful girl who had nothing else but beauty going for her, will have nothing in her older years when her beauty is "taken away" by society.

Even though beauty has been important to women and is equated with sexuality, women have been more sexually repressed than men in their family structure. The extent of the repression varies, but it is obvious, even in old age, when the option of masturbating, for instance, is presented as a possibility for those who are alone. It is evident, too, with the female reaction to self breast examination or a gynecological self-exam. All of these activities bring women face to face with basic cultural taboos about their bodies and confront them with the negative attitudes in which they have been socialized since infancy.

Most women, especially those who are older, think of their genitals as unclean, smelly, and ugly. This is hardly surprising considering that women have been taught to think that way since childhood. Most have very negative images of their bodies. Think of the difference between little boys and little girls in toilet training. Little boys are complimented if they just hit the mark. Little girls, on the other hand, are admonished to wipe themselves clean. Right away they are given the message that they are dirty. Little brother just shakes his penis dry and puts it back in his pants. Sister, on the other hand, must use a wad of paper to protect her hands from the dirty urine that for some reason, although she's not quite sure why, is dirtier between her legs than it is on her brother's penis.

Growing older, boys have locker room conversations about their genitals, have no stalls or cubicles to undress and urinate in, and learn to talk openly about their bodies. Girls learn, instead, to hide themselves and certainly not talk about their genitals with each other because that would be terrible. They know that anything too terrible to talk about must *really* be awful. This, then, confirms earlier training about unclean genitals. I wonder, in fact, how many girls consciously failed to wash that part between their legs because it would be risky to touch something so unclean. Or perhaps they were admonished by an older relative who caught them in the bath tub or shower actually "touching" there and were made to feel very, very guilty.

This, then, is the extra baggage that women have brought with them into their sexual encounters. Many women today have had sexual intercourse, borne several babies, been examined by gynecologists, and yet have never looked at their own genitals, nor touched them, unless something intervened between that dirty, ugly place and their fingers. This is why, when suggesting to an older woman that masturbation is an alternative, it is important to keep in mind that she may not be able to touch her genitals. When that happens a vibrator or some other object (even an electric toothbrush) can be suggested so that she need not touch herself until she can become comfortable doing so.

It is easy to see how the relationship between elders and society and the latter's negative cues have had a strong impact on the self-concept of our older people. Sexuality is an integral aspect of one's self-concept. Since society prescribes sexlessness—and most of our older citizens were raised to respect the dictates of society—they take this prescription too well, and often without question. They struggle hard to learn behaviors that will hide their sexuality. Could that be why a mother who was usually a well-dressed, stylish lady changes to a drab, unkept old woman who isolates herself from others and protects herself from negative reactions?

Finally, the strength of cultural expectations is made even more obvious by a reported study of 106 cultures.[4] Many of these cultures have expectations for continued sexual activity of older men and women and, as can be expected, that activity flourishes. Interestingly, many of these reports showed an expectation for greater sexual activity on the part of older women than older men. Sure enough, that is exactly what happened. Doesn't this show very clearly the strong affect cultural expectations have on sexual behavior?

NOTES

1. C. Gordon and G. Johnson (eds.), *Readings in Human Sexuality: Contemporary Perspectives* (New York: Harper and Row, 1976), 34-37.
2. J. N. D. Kelly, *Early Christian Doctrines*, 2nd ed. (New York: Harper and Row, 1960), 364-65.
3. Schneider in C. Gordon and G. Johnson (eds.), *Readings in Human Sexuality: Contemporary Perspectives*, op. cit., 48-51.
4. R. Winn and N. Newton, "Sexuality in Aging: A Study of 106 Cultures," *Archives of Sexual Behavior* 11 (1982): 283-98.

3

Developmental Sexuality
Change Throughout the Decades

"Elderly men should not marry. Remember that virility is essential to produce healthy, vigorous offspring. Old men have, unless in rare cases, lost much of their virility. One noted writer claims that the cause of the increasing number of diseases and weaknesses of our generation is the growing tendency to postpone marriage until time or indulgence has diminished the forces and exposed the system to succumb readily to any unusual drain upon its resources."

Eugenics, 1915

Developmental psychology indicates to us that we develop cognitively, emotionally, and socially throughout life. This concurs with the relatively new view that, in fact, we stop changing, as indicated in the psychology textbooks we studied as late as the 1970s. Study of human development used to stop at adulthood, but now we know that there are many and varied changes beyond that time. One such change is sexual devlopment. Although research findings on sexual activity in later life provide some view of what is common in advanced adulthood, we still do not know enough about normal changes in sexuality. A life span theory of sexuality should be consistent with other life span developmental changes. It is reasonable to expect considerable continuity over the life span in sexuality, just as in other areas of development; however, there are always variations and individual differences.[1] It is important for the reader to keep in mind that what is learned about sexuality throughout life may be true for most older people yet different for the particular family member under consideration. This potential for variation exists for the reader as well.

There are three different aspects of early sexuality. The first is the development of our fundamental identity as male or female, which is taught very early and learned both thoroughly and well. For instance, we learn by the assignment of our given name that we are male or female. The second aspect is the learning of social determinants, the current set of rules, about what is masculine and what is feminine. Some deviation is permitted, but not much. If we move or explore beyond permitted boundaries, we are labeled and responded to as being "deviant." Third, heterosexuality and homosexuality differ from the first two aspects and are treated as separate phenomena. Styles of behavior (heterosexual and homosexual) are established in our fantasies and we carry these throughout adult life. They provide us with much of what is called our sense of identity.

Personal identity, from approximately age two onward, has been interwoven with sexual identity. If we feel we are taken out of our sex roles or are functioning less sexually, it is not only our bodies, but our image of ourselves, that is affected. From infancy we are stroked, hugged, kissed, and held. We learn to respond by doing the same in return. By old age, though, we may be isolated and deprived of this very important part of our sense of self.[2]

In infancy and early childhood females have a greater growth-rate than males. They mature physically approximately two years earlier than their male counterparts and are often bigger and stronger, until puberty. They actually have greater genetic protection against disease and environmental stress and yet are thought of, and treated, as being fragile. Young girls are made to feel dependent through an overemphasis on protection and restrictions placed on their participation in strenuous physical activity.[3] Learning of gender role differences is so powerful that differences in behavior have been noted within the first year. Girls are less physically active but are more in tune with environmental stimuli. Some think that this reduced physical activity contributes at a very early age to girls being more aware of social demands, more willing to live up to the wishes of their parents, and more likely to be rewarded for being dependent and "good little girls." As a result, girls learn early on that their self-worth is based upon pleasing others, most especially male others. Nurturing and accommodating behavior are quickly internalized; females learn that the most important goal in life is to be loved, and the easiest way to be loved is by being very, very "good."[4] Girls learn that they are made of "sugar and spice and everything nice," while boys learn that they are made of "snips and snails and puppy dog tails." That's pretty powerful stuff to lay on a two-year-old! Did you learn that "There was a little girl, who had a little curl, right in the middle of her forehead. When she was good, she was very very good, but when she was bad, she was horrid"? That admonition is alive and well in all the women who heard it as a child.

Fairy tales and nursery rhymes, those timeless escapes into fantasy, provide girls with a picture of themselves as helpless creatures, always being protected and taken care of. When Jack fell down and broke his crown, could Jill carry on and get the water? Of course not! She was so distressed that she just simply came tumbling down after him. Perhaps the most negative image in these fairy tales and nursery rhymes is that of the older woman, usually depicted as a witch, an evil stepmother, or such a prolific bearer of children that she didn't know what to do—poor soul.

The textbooks that girls and boys read continue to influence their lives well after moving on to another grade level. Of the well-known trio of Dick, Jane, and Spot, usually Spot, the dog, had more ideas about what to do than Jane, who just stood there looking pretty and watching it all. But it has been suggested that Jane now has a sister named Sue, and that is exactly what women are now doing, "sueing" for such things as equal pay and to halt sexual harassment.[5]

Ours is not the only society that promotes the image of girls as being "good." Most cultures encourage nurturing behavior in their females. This emphasis is an important behavior difference between boys and girls in that it is believed to delay the moral development of girls, since more emphasis is placed upon feelings and relationships than on the group expectations for conforming behavior, that males come to value.

There are significant gender differences in children's thinking about things sexual. Parents give selective information based upon the sex of their child as loving and protective attitudes are reinforced. Girls begin to place more emphasis on romantic love, and boys on companionship. The ultimate horror concerning the emphasis on girls being loving, giving, and nurturing, is most seriously presented in the incidence of child abuse. It is estimated that one out of every four girls in our country will be sexually abused in some way before reaching the age of eighteen.[6] How does a girl protect herself from, or refuse, a caregiving adult who is the source of her rewards, self-esteem, and of love itself? She has been conditioned to please. Isn't this the ultimate way of pleasing? Very early in life a woman is given the message of just who she is sexually and exactly what is expected of her.

How is the sexual development of little boys affected? Within the first three days of life 90 percent of male infants in our country are circumcised.[7] Contrast this with only 5 percent in Great Britain. It is thought that this is one of the greatest traumas faced in life, second only to the trauma of birth. A recent study indicates that, whereas boys have been identified as crying more than girls in the first few months of life, male infants who are uncircumcised exhibit no greater crying behavior than female infants. Circumcision continues despite expert opinion that it not be a routine procedure, a stand taken by the American Academy of Pediatrics, the Pediatric Urologist Association, and the American College of Obstetricians and Gynecologists. The contention is that the procedure began only for religious reasons, and it was not until the late 1880s that the surgical procedure was used to improve sexuality and prevent masturbation and venereal disease. All other reasons related to the prevention of ills or improving sexuality should be relegated to myth until scientific evidence is forthcoming. So far, this stand has resulted in little substantive change in our country, but my guess is that we will begin to notice a change as insurance companies drop the practice from their list of covered procedures, as has been done in Great Britain.

Early childhood is a crucial time for developing body image. Interestingly, children of nudists, or of parents who accept nudity in the home, avoid these negative images as adults and measure higher in self-esteem than do those individuals who were raised in homes where nudity was not allowed.

Boys have a more difficult time developing role models. Often they do not see much of their father and, when they do, he may not be doing much around the house that the male child can copy. In school there are many female roles but few male, except perhaps the principal, the physical education teacher, and the janitor. The male child is not sure what the principal does, he begins to wonder why the physical education teacher isn't coaching a high school team, and all he knows about the janitor is that he operates out of a closet filled with mops and brooms. As a result, males are more insecure than females about their gender roles and thus cling more strongly to stereotypical male behavior. Males are therefore more distrustful of females than females are of males; little boys actually develop a feeling of hostility toward girls—"girls, yuck!" This rigidity and difficulty with their gender role leads to problems of gender identification and sexual health, as evidenced by transvestism and the high incidence of males who engage in fetishism and paraphilias.

Throughout the elementary school years, boys develop rigid control of their behavior in order not to be labeled as "sissy," with its dreaded implication of homosexuality. This is the root of homophobia (intense negative feelings toward homosexuals) so strongly felt by the American male, whereas it is felt to a much lesser degree in the female. As a result, many boys (with strong urging and support from their parents) push themselves into every sport available. They know that their parents, and their teachers, will forgive any lack of school achievement as long as they hit the winning home run. They do benefit, however, from the competition these sports provide. It allows them to make game-losing mistakes and shows them that life goes on anyway. Boys are also more likely to involve themselves in other forms of competition, such as debating teams, running for class offices, or participating in scholastic teams vying against other schools. Girls, on the other hand, do not often take the chance to fail in public and, as a result, become very poor risk-takers, a fact that lowers their achievement level. As an elementary school teacher for many years, I learned that if I wanted the right answer immediately, I needed to call on a girl, even one with hand raised tentatively, for she would have the correct answer. The five boys, waving their hands madly and confidently, may or may not. They knew a wrong answer would not devastate them, while a wrong answer from a girl might reduce her to tears. Young boys and girls thus carry with them into their older years much more behavioral learning than the memorized facts they hope to retain for a test.

One thing boys do learn in school is that they are important, although they are not quite certain why. What girls learn in school is that they are *not* important and, therefore, they had better plan on marrying someone who *is* important. Although this is changing, it was all too true for the older adults we are talking about in this book.

Sex hormone production increases dramatically for both sexes at puberty. In highly industrialized societies like ours, the increased energy this produces is not channeled into either uninhibited sexual gratification or productive work activities. This is one of the causes of the high suicide rate, especially for male adolescents. Many students admit that one of their most serious problems at that time in their lives was related to their sudden sexual urges, and they had no one to talk to. What a shame that voters in our school districts do not provide the necessary funds to hire enough guidance counselors to do more than assign classes and help with college and job plans!

The discrepancy between sexual drive and gratification differs for men and women throughout the life cycle. Men are most potent in their late teens and early twenties while women seldom achieve their sexual high point until their thirties, probably the result of sexual repression experienced during childhood and adolescence.[8] Interestingly, the age at which women experience heightened sexual response is lowering, which indicates a lessening of this repression.

The sexual script for many adolescent girls is to be independent, sexual, but always acceptable. No wonder they feel confused, helpless, and depressed, given how difficult it is to act out their script.

At adolescence, females experience their first menstrual period along with other changes of a maturing body. They are concerned about body image, relationships, values, and decisions made about their sexual behavior, in addition to goals for the future. The challenge is to become independent of the childhood role with parents and to seek one's own identity. This is done in the context of both female and male peer group valuing of women who are physically attractive and both socially and sexually conforming. Conflict arises because the personal need for independence is undermined not only by social needs but by its rewards for being dependent. Females may feel overwhelmed, powerless, and angry as they look at their choices: being promiscous/nonpromiscuous and achieving the goal of a career/wife/mother.

Unplanned pregnancy and eating disorders are not unlikely results. Both are evidence of confusion over sexuality, body image, autonomy, and self-esteem. Those with eating disorders seem to be struggling with issues related to control and dependency. Women who become pregnant and/or promiscuous struggle with the inability to risk the withdrawal of what they thought to be the love of an important male figure and their need to do what pleased others. Some young woman view pregnancy as an attractive alternative to their problems, having a "doll" baby of their very own to love and to love them, but not realizing the enormity of the different set of problems this produces.

Male sexual development is more genital (presocial) while that of females is more social. Masturbation for boys contributes to this as they begin conscious masturbatory activity earlier than girls and engage in it more frequently. The majority are aware of parental or societal disapproval so they do it alone and silently, rarely in groups. This hardly develops the interpersonal relationship training needed later on. When adolescent boys realize that their culture views masturbation as childish and a poor substitute for "the real thing," they are pressured into sexual intercourse.[9] This is reflected in the content of adolescent male fantasies, where the conquest is the thing, and the sexual release the object. Female fantasies, meanwhile, revolve around romantic love, their wedding day, and a rose-covered cottage.

The lack of a uniform mechanism for sex education has an enormous effect on males. They are expected to be all-knowing in areas of sexual information and performance, whereas standardized tests show them to be far behind girls. At the college and graduate level, young men enroll in human sexuality courses in small numbers. This causes communication gaps and a lack of mutual sharing of sexual problems between males and females. Lack of information leads to obvious health problems.

As adolescent males struggle with their sexual identity, the homophobia engendered in childhood causes them to over-react to any suggestion of their own possible homosexuality, or that of male friends. Therefore they avoid any impulse toward same-sex intimacy such as hugging or touching. Homophobia becomes the most effective control of male behavior and interferes with any expression of caring. This is believed to result in serious mental health problems for boys. They are seen in mental health clinics three times as often as girls; they outnumber girls in mental institutions by 150 percent; boys are six times more likely to be involved with narcotics; and they fall victim to three times more suicides.

In adulthood, the influence on women of gaining self-esteem through accommodating males and authority figures continues to influence their sexual health. Women, the majority of whom work outside the home, earn less money than men and continue to have the main responsibility for childcare and homecare. Their increased incidence of smoking, heart disease, and alcoholism has been associated with stress.[10] Interestingly, this stress is not felt as greatly by women executives but rather by those who feel powerless in their jobs. But even these women report less illness than homemakers.

During adulthood the tide has turned, with more women than men suffering from physical as well as emotional illness. This may be because more women are willing to reveal their illness, recognize symptoms, and take action. Women are four times more likely than men to be treated for depression, which classically results from directing anger inward at oneself rather than outward at others. Diminished self-esteem is involved, and it may be that middle-aged women have finally accommodated more than they can or want to. Psychotropic (mood altering) drugs are used more often by women than men, and women use more physician and hospital services and have more surgical procedures performed than their male counterparts. The unanswered question is if these surgical procedures are really necessary and if a woman's "need to please" and to defer to the authority figure is so powerful that she will relinquish power over her own health and body. If a woman visits a male physician, she will rarely interrupt to ask a question or make a comment; however, she will do so if the physician is a female. Along this line, it is interesting to mention that, during conversations, women are interrupted more often by men (95 percent).

A friend of mine visited her gynecologist, a woman, and a diagnostic dilation/curretage (D&C) was recommended. After my friend made the gynecologist aware of her extensive health-related background, it soon became just as appropriate to opt for a lesser procedure, a biopsy, in order to provide the needed information. Perhaps it is not only male physicians who are at fault for unnecessary surgical procedures. The inability of women to carry out self-examination techniques—a fact rooted in entrenched attitudes about sexuality and control over health—results in their inability effectively to prevent the incidence of uterine and breast cancer, the leading causes of death for women between the ages of thirty-five and fifty-four.

For adult men, one of the most clearly gender-linked concerns is the health of the prostate gland, about which more will be said in chapter 9 where health issues are discussed in greater detail. This particular part of the male anatomy is associated more than any other with myth and misinformation. There may be a bacterial cause for prostate problems, but usually they are associated with (a) infrequent sexual activity, (b) irregular sexual activity, or (c) hyperactive sexual activity. This is a classic damned-if-you-do, damned-if-you-don't situation. What males can do is keep a calendar record of their own sexual activity for three to six months and arrive at the frequency that is comfortable for them rather than worrying about statistical norms and keeping up with the Joneses. A regular sex life, based upon what is good for the individual, is the best safeguard against prostate problems and helps to extend healthy sexual expression well into old age.[11]

Acquired Immune Deficiency Syndrome (AIDS) is the newest and most deadly disease to affect society generally but most predominantly the male population. Although the majority of males who have thus far tested positive for the AIDS virus are homosexual or bisexual, the disease is expanding its reach into the heterosexual community. Until there is a vaccine to provide immunity, the best medical advice is to reduce the number of sexual partners, avoid sexual behavior where blood or semen is exchanged, use condoms, and substitute with masturbation or affectional intimacy rather than sexual intimacy.

Men will typically ignore signs of illness as they continue to play the role of "being a man." As a result they are hospitalized 15 percent longer than women for the same disease or condition and make fewer visits to physicians. They are less likely to seek help for mental health problems, or therapy for any kind of sexual dysfunction. Since they have difficulty expressing feelings, there is a greater incidence of hypertension leading to strokes, renal disease, and peptic ulcers. Of the ten leading causes of death, only diabetes is not linked in some way with the masculine role.[12]

Physical and emotional health affect the sexual responses of males earlier and more directly than is the case with women. Illness, strain, and anxiety lower the levels of the male hormone testosterone. The present picture for male sexual health is rather dismal and can only be improved with earlier education in sexuality and drastic changes in the socialization patterns of men. Unfortunately, even older men, to whom we ascribe maturity, have not gained adequate knowledge of sexual health or the wisdom to use it.

A recurring theme in the relevant literature depicts sexual enjoyment as a capacity developed early and one that can be maintained throughout life. There are physiological changes, but psychological elements are probably far more consequential in determining the character of older people's sex lives.

The Duke Longitudinal Studies have provided us with much needed data on sexual functioning in the middle and later years. Some generalizations of these results follow: (1) The older one gets the less heterosexual activity takes place, although men are more active than women at any age. (2) Sexual activity (especially among males) seems to decline sharply in the mid-seventies with the onset of debilitating illness. (3) The older the person the lower degree of sexual interest. (4) Decreasing sexual activity and interest patterns occur earlier for women than for men. (5) Both men and women report awareness of sexual decline. (6) Cessation of sexual activity was primarily the result of male dysfunction (e.g., inability to achieve or maintain an erection, losing interest in sex, being too ill to engage in the sex act). (7) Marital status made a great difference in the sexual activity level for women, but much less for men.[13]

Developmentally, changes do occur in women that can affect their sexuality. Changes in the genitals occur during the years after menopause. These include a gradual shrinking and atrophying of the uterus and constriction of the vaginal lining. Vaginal secretions that lubricate in anticipation of and during intercourse may diminish, resulting in pain (dyspareunia) during intercourse. There may be vaginal burning and itching. All of this sounds awful, but most women feel no discomfort and those who do simply need to see a physician for suggested treatment.

With respect to emotional changes in women as they age, there are several reasons to explain older women feeling more sexual: (1) the elimination of any concern about pregnancy; (2) the children are reared and thus no longer likely to intrude on intimate moments; (3) the lower response of an aging partner may afford women more time for sexual pleasuring; and (4) there is an increase in time and energy available to the couple, especially after retirement.[14]

Some women, however, use the "excuse" of menopause or advancing years to avoid the personal embarrassment of what they are afraid is inadequate sexual performance. They may also be experiencing the frustration of unresolved sexual tensions. However, in nearly all instances of actual cessation of sexual intercourse, the responsibility rests with the male.

Men have more opportunity to satisfy their sexuality as they age: if married, they may opt for extramarital partners; if single or unattached, they can "play the field." In any case, however, they often feel the need to meet certain standards of performance, standards better suited for men thirty years their junior.

We often hear the term "male menopause" bandied about, but there really is no male condition (emotional or physical) that corresponds to female menopause. The male testes continue to function, although there is a gradual decline in the rate of testosterone and of sperm production. Men can continue to father children, but since the sperm count is lower, fertilization is not as frequent. Erectile impotence affects one of every four males at age seventy, whereas it affects only one percent of males at age thirty-five.[14] The correlation between aging and impotence, however, is not inevitable. It is important to remember that psychologically induced impotence can be treated, and several devices have been perfected to allow an erection for a man with physiologically induced impotence.

At around age sixty, men have an average of slightly less than one copulation with orgasm per week, whereas those age fifteen to twenty average four per week. The frequency of morning erections drops steadily with age. More stimulation is necessary to produce an erection and more time is needed to produce a second erection. A young man may be able to have a second erection almost immediately, whereas an older male might take up to twenty-four hours.[15] The force of the ejaculate is less and, therefore, may cause a decrease in sensation. There is also some decline of erotic response to sexual stimulation (those calendar girls don't excite as quickly or as intensely anymore). The older male may have a tendency to be more absorbed in work than in sex, until he retires. But then, look out! Often he will experience a renewed sexual drive once his work pressures are behind him.

There is no biological imperative for a sudden end to sexual activity. Overall reduction in vigor and strength may decrease sexual capacity but it does not result in an end to sexual activity for either men or women. Those who were most sexually active in their younger years will continue to be the most sexually active as they grow older. A comparison of the sexual response of the young and the aging male, as well as the young and aging female, appears in the Appendix.

Popular misconceptions about the needs and desires of older people continue to flourish, in spite of evidence to the contrary. It is the older people themselves who are becoming more vocal about the denial of their sexuality. It is doubtful they can ever escape the values of their own upbringing, but some are beginning to look at the possibilities that have been part of the sexual experience of other age groups, such as cohabitation, group living arrangements, and homosexual relationships.

NOTES

1. Catherine G. Adams and Barbara F. Turner, "Reported Change in Sexuality from Young Adulthood to Old Age," *Journal of Sex Research* 21 (May 1985): 126-41.

2. Carlfred Broderick in R. L. Solnick (ed.) *Sexuality and Aging* (Los Angeles: The University of Southern California Press, 1978), 1-8.

3. B. Yorburg, *Sexual Identity* (New York: Wiley Interscience Books, 1974), 45.

4. Ann Welbourne-Maglia and Deryck Calderwood, "Gender, Gender Role, and Sexual Health," in annual editions of *Human Sexuality*, edited by Ollie Pocs (Guilford, Conn.: Dushkin Publishing Group, 1986), 48-51.

5. Morris Massey, "What You Are Is What You Were When," video presentation, (Farmington Hills, Mich.: Magnetic Video Library, 1981).

6. Welbourne-Maglia and Calderwood, op. cit., 49.

7. Ibid., 48.

8. Yorburg, op. cit.

9. Welbourne-Maglia and Calderwood, op. cit.

10. Ibid., 49.

11. Ibid., 51.

12. Ibid.

13. E. Pfeiffer, A. Verwoerdt, and G. C. Dairs, "Sexual Behavior in Middle Life," *American Journal of Psychiatry* 128 (1972): 82-87.

14. H. A. Katchadourian and D. T. Lund, *Fundamentals of Human Sexuality*, 2nd ed. (New York: Holt Rinehart and Winston, 1975), 371.

15. B. J. Sadock, H. I. Kaplan, and A. M. Friedman, *The Sexual Experience* (Baltimore: The Williams and Wilkins Co., 1976).

4

Menopause and Mid-Life

Crisis or Challenge?

"During and after the change of life, it is also important to observe an unwanted moderation. During that period any unaccustomed excitement of this character may be followed by flooding and other serious symptoms, while after the crisis has been passed, the sexual appetite itself should wholly or almost wholly disappear."

Eugenics, 1915

It is time for the mystery to be taken out of menopause (what is commonly referred to as the change of life). Every woman approaches menopause uncertain of just what her own reactions and experiences will be. I know this to be true from the workshops and small groups conducted to help women through the psychological adjustment. Mainly, these women just need information about something that is a natural part of life. They know so little about menopause that it confirms in many minds the existence of a shroud of mystery. Along with menopause, there are always questions about mid-life as well. We will therefore deal first with menopause, followed by a general discussion of both women and men at mid-life. Is there a mid-life crisis? Does it occur at the same time and in the same way for both men and women?

Our discussion of menopause will be directed to every reader: the young, who wonder what their mothers are experiencing; and the old, who can look back on their own experiences in the context of what it was like for others. Women who are experiencing menopause, or are about to, will find this discussion especially meaningful, as will their husbands, who could benefit from a greater understanding of this very normal stage in the lives of their mates.

The workshops I conducted were offered by Planned Parenthood, an organization long thought to be interested only in younger women's sexual concerns. It is gratifying to know that older women's issues are receiving recognition as well. This is another indication that society has begun to adjust its thinking and its programs to meet the needs of the fastest growing population group. The workshops are in two parts: physiological and psychological. It is importrant to have a strong physiological base from which to begin discussion.

What is commonly understood by "menopause" is the final cessation of menses (the cyclical expulsion of the uterine lining in preparation for the presence of an egg), whereas the term "climateric" refers to the entire transitional period during which the reproductive function is diminished and lost. During menopause the ovaries stop producing eggs, so the levels of estrogen and progesterone, the female hormones, drop. The pituitary gland, no longer held in check by the ovarian hormones, attempts to stimulate the ovary and trigger ovulation.

Usually the ovary gears down slowly. A woman may ovulate one month but not the next. Periods may be skipped a month or two and then start up again; some women may menstruate normally and then stop abruptly. All of this is perfectly normal and nothing to be concerned about. However, should a woman stop for a year or so and then start again; have a heavy, gushing flow; or experience periods that last longer than usual or occur at more frequent intervals than twenty-one days; she should consult a physician.

Eventually the periods stop altogether. This used to be at an average age of forty-eight, but that age is increasing and it is no longer unusual for women to still be menstruating in their mid-fifties, with a very a few continuing into their sixth decade. It is thought that this may be due to better nutrition.[1] We do know that there is a correlation between mothers and daughters with respect to the time of menopause but it is uncertain whether this is genetic or simply the result of similar nutritional and enviromental causes.

Climateric women may experience various changes at this time. It seems that everyone has heard of hot flashes (or flushes), which are short episodes of profuse sweating and a feeling of intense heat. Also a thinning of the vaginal and urinary tissues may occur, leaving both more susceptible to infections and potential pain during intercourse. Osteoporosis (the loss of bone density) may cause greater susceptibility to fractures. All of these conditions seem to be related to changing hormonal levels.

Hot flashes seem to be the most frequently talked about, perhaps because of their descriptive name. They usually begin as a feeling of heat in the chest and spread to the neck and head. Sometimes the entire body is affected. The skin may become bright red. After perspiring profusely, a woman may become chilled. The flash may last from a few seconds to several minutes, and may occur several times a day or only once or twice a week. Approximately 65 percent of women experience hot flashes but only one in five suffer serious problems. Some women have them so frequently during the night that insomnia may result. The flashes rarely continue longer than a year and sometimes are very short-lived.[2]

What causes the hot flash? Vessels dilate causing blood to rush to the surface of the skin. Why this happens, no one knows exactly. Just as mysteriously, the blood vessels return to their former state and the symptoms subside. Some medical researchers believe that hot flashes are caused by lower levels of estrogen, while other experts feel they are caused by high levels of pituitary hormones.

The decline in levels of estrogen causes a thinning of the vaginal, vulvar, and urinary tissues. This can result in dryness and itching. The thinning of the vaginal walls may produce a vaginal discharge, a condition known as postmenopausal vaginitis. The reduction in vaginal lubrication may be a source of pain during intercourse. The thinning of the urinary and vag nal tissues is associated with a falling down (prolapse) of the urinary organs. The decline in estrogen may alter the acid/alkaline balance of the vagina, thus making women more susceptible to infections.

As indicated earlier, another condition that may be associated with menopause is osteoporosis, resulting from lower levels of estrogen. Much attention has been given to this condition of late, wherein bone density is decreased. Some people may have osteoporosis without experiencing any problems at all. Others may be very susceptible to bone (especially hip) fractures. When a woman breaks her hip, it's often not known if this was caused by a fall, or if the bone fractured on its own, causing a fall. There have been cases of older women just turning over in bed and fracturing a bone.

It is not clear if osteoporosis is directly related to menopause and to decreased estrogen levels. There is evidence that other factors, such as lack of exercise, lack of calcium in the diet, and smoking are related to this condition. It may be that lower levels of estrogen indirectly affect the way the body uses nutrients, making a woman more susceptible to the condition. The uncertain association of osteoporosis with menopause or estrogen deprivation has caused controversy with respect to appropriate treatment options.

Some people think weight gain is associated with menopause but it is not an estrogen-related phenomenon. Rather, women in this age group tend to exercise less, while failing to adjust their caloric intake. Speaking of weight, it is interesting to note that those menopausal women who exhibit the most severe symptoms are usually described as thin. It may be that body weight has more to do with the severity of menopausal symptoms than any set of psychological factors. This may sound far-fetched and has not been thoroughly researched, but women who pass through menopause with barely any lowered level of estrogen tend to have more body weight. We know that certain substances can be converted to estrogen in the fatty tissues of the body.[3] In our body conscious society, it is always rewarding to hear something positive about being fat.

The question to be addressed is: what can be done about these menopausal changes? Concerning efforts to relieve the discomfort of hot flashes, some of the best answers come from women themselves:

1. Wear lightweight clothing, such as cotton. A menopause wardrobe should include loose blouses and jackets.
2. If hot flashes occur during the night, kick off the covers. Wear

lightweight pajamas, or sleep in the nude.

3. Carry moistened towelettes with you.
4. Go easy on heavy makeup.
5. Keep the house cool.
6. Eat frequent, small meals.
7. Go easy on caffeine and alcohol.
8. Drink cool water or juice after exercise.

If vaginal lubrication has started to decrease, use a lubricating jelly. Lubrication is usually not a problem for women who are sexually active over fairly regular intervals. Vaginal tissue responds to being stimulated regularly, whether through intercourse or masturbation.

The reduction of muscular tension in the pelvic area, which may result in some minor "leakage," especially when a woman laughs or sneezes, can be alleviated by the use of "Kegal" exercises that involve the vaginal and pelvic muscles. Kegel exercises involve using the same muscle used to stop yourself while urinating. This muscle needs to be flexed several times during the day—while driving the car or talking on the phone, for instance. This exercise will also increase vaginal tone.

Any discussion of treatment for menopausal symptoms must involve a discussion of estrogen therapy. One woman told Planned Parenthood that she experienced some discomfort but felt that she could live through the hot flashes and night sweats. However, her gynecologist suggested that she take estrogen to replace the hormone her body was no longer making. She had never taken many pills and was reluctant to start on estrogen, so she checked with her family doctor. To her surprise, she found him to be as negative about the idea as her gynecologist was positive. The general practitioner told her that estrogen replacement might cause a greater risk of cancer, heart attack, or stroke.

Now she *really* didn't know what to do, so she sought a third opinion, that of an internist. He reassured her that the risk of uterine cancer can be reduced by the addition of progestin (another female hormone) to the estrogen treatment. This would also reduce the risk of heart attack and could protect her from osteoporosis. Even though it still bothers her that the physicians disagreed, she opted for the estrogen/progestin treatment.

Millions of women are faced with this quandary. During the 1960s estrogen was oversold as a way to keep "feminine forever." There was hardly a mention of side effects. Then, in the 1970s, it seemed all that we women heard about was the danger of side effects from ingesting estrogen. Research has piled up since then, but all the results aren't clear. It does appear, however, that adding a ten- to fourteen-day dose of progestin gets around the increased risk of uterine or breast cancer. Although doctors still do not agree, it seems that women at high risk might opt for this newer form of estrogen therapy.

The psychological effects of menopause are not directly caused by the event itself, but rather by how we think about it. In therapy groups, I will often use Dr. Albert Ellis's *ABC* method (Rational Emotive Therapy) to point this out. Here's how it works: *A* is the *A*ctivating Event (in this case, menopause); *B* is our *B*elief system (e.g., "I feel awful because . . . I have lost a symbol of femininity. . .)," *C* is the *C*onsequence (e.g., "I will never feel good again"; "my life is over"; "I wish I were dead," . . .).

The goal is to take a hard look at our belief systems and to recognize what *what we believe* about an activating event (menopause), not the event itself, is what causes the consequence (i.e., "my life is over"). By consciously changing our belief system to "I feel good because I don't have to wear a tampon anymore" or "Menopause may mean I am older, but I *choose* not to let that make me feel bad," a woman can change the consequence.

Some women do report feeling depressed after menopause, but what they really seem to feel is a sense of loss, whether real or perceived. When we know we are looking at the second half of life, we may tend to look too longingly at what might have been and start counting the losses instead of the gains. We may feel time is running out to fulfill the dreams we thought we could always accomplish "next year." Then, too, we may have begun to experience losses through death. The death of friends or family seem to occur more steadly than before. Whatever the cause, the feeling of loss and how it is associated in our minds with menopause is what causes the depression, not menopause itself.

We all feel depressed at times and, even though we feel we should be able to (and often can) control our own thoughts, there may be times when counseling is in order. If prolonged periods of depression render a woman unable to function as she did before, then there may be a chemical imbalance involved, perhaps even brought on by the depression itself. It is possible for the nervous system to malfunction, just like other parts of her body, and medical help may be needed.

Irrational attitudes and misinformation about menopause may cause some mental problems. A woman may consider the event to be so catastrophic that she refuses to have sex with her husband, complains about everything, and acts as though she is waiting to die. Obviously, this will cause a severe strain on her relationship with her sexual partner, her family, and her friends.

Some women overcompensate for menopause by trying too hard to "regain their youth." They run the gamut trying everything: exercise, diet, cosmetic treatments, partying, drinking, flirting, and, in doing so, they appear to act rather silly. Fortunately, most women don't fall into this pattern. The character of Mrs. Robinson in the 1967 film *The Graduate* is an example of a middle-aged woman who reacted to the inhibitions of her youth by making up for lost time.

Generally the woman who has successfully gone through changes in her life and has not been too dependent on others, will go through menopause almost without realizing it has occurred. Also, the busy woman, the woman who has outside activities to think about, will generally have little that is negative to say about menopause.

A survey conducted by *Family Circle* magazine (1985) looked at reactions to menopause.[4] It was found that two-thirds of the respondents felt that it wasn't too stressful. Some women did recall their mothers' bad experiences and were fearful that they, too, might have the same reactions, but most viewed menopause as a natural life occurrence to be dealt with like other changes, such as menstruation and pregnancy. Three quarters of the survey felt just as womanly, attractive, and happily married as before. One-third said they felt *more* relaxed, and one in five felt *more* self-confident. Almost half the respondents said that menopause did not change their relationships with their husbands; they felt even closer or more comfortable with their spouses. More than half considered their husbands to be more helpful during menopause than a doctor, a friend, or a relative. Six out of ten wives said they were not depressed, the majority of whom attributed this to the fact that they had satisfying marriages. Other positives and negatives from the survey: 44 percent gained weight, 32 percent felt freer and more in control of their lives, 25 percent noticed a decrease in sexual desire, 20 percent enjoyed sex more, 17 percent enjoyed sex less.

Another survey, by Edward M. Brecher, published in Consumer Reports Books,[5] contained some interesting comments about menopause. According to a sixty-nine-year-old widow: "Menopause increased my sexual enjoyment because of not having to worry about getting pregnant—there was no birth control pill before I reached menopausal age." A fifty-four-year-old wife remarked: "It is great not getting pregnant or having monthly bothers." And a fifty-one-year-old wife said: "Menopause has brought with it a new freedom in sex with my spouse—as well as a feeling of control of my life and a new spurt of energy, never having those 'tired days.' I love it! Also, I have had a group of women for the past three years in a creative maturity group, exploring life's changes and (now) we can grow in more ways."

One creative person decided to have a party. She intends to call it a "Menopause Gala" to mark her liberation from the tyranny of menstruation. She said she will serve *hot* and *cold* hors d'oeuvres in honor of the "flashes" and she'll toast not only marshmallows, but birth control devices as well, over a bonfire. Along with this, she'll serve Bloody Marys. Perhaps, after all, a sense of humor is the best way to deal with this change.[6]

Menopause is not really a mid-life crisis. It comes far too late for that, at least for women. Gail Sheehy, in her best selling book *Passages*, says that women hit their mid-life crisis around the age of thirty-five. She calls this a crossroads. It is at approximately this age that the average woman sends her last child off to school; begins the dangerous age of infidelity; reenters the work force; if divorced, she takes a new husband; becomes a runaway wife; and brings her biological boundry (i.e., menopause) into sight.[7]

Of course, men cannot experience menopause, having never menstruated, and they rarely confront a sudden physical change. Much has been written about the male climateric as though men could take hormonal therapy to control the changes occurring at their mid-life. Such a need seems rare indeed. Actually, most men do seem to experience a mid-life crisis, but this is usually when they are in their early forties and its occurrence results from psychological factors.

A major reason for this mid-life crisis is that, by the age of forty, a man has been working approximately twenty years. He may not have achieved the position in the company he thought he would have, or he may be bored. He may have begun to feel like just a "meal ticket" at home. Feeling a perceived lack of appreciation, he begins to seek change in his life.

The mid-life man may search for change in several ways: drinking too much; staying out late; making frequent or radical changes in his job or appearance; or he may have an extramarital relationship. Often the relationship is with a much younger woman, whom Sheehy calls the "testimonial woman." She is a testimony to his youth. She adores him. Why shouldn't she? His wife, who has known him over the years, looks at him and sees all the "baggage" he has brought with him during their lifetime together. The testimonial woman sees him, instead, as a well-dressed, successful, take-charge kind of person. She feeds into his ego needs at a time when his ego is at its lowest. It is easy to see why the relationship may flourish, at least for a while.

For both men and women the middle years can be seen as either a cup half empty or a cup half full. Middle-agers can look at these years either in negative ways or as a beginning to the second half of life, filled with much to accomplish and to enjoy. If one thinks about all that has happened during the first half, it should be exciting to imagine that every bit as much can happen in the second half.

Along with physical changes that occur as normal components of aging, difficult family situations may occur: separation, divorce, or the death of a spouse. These can lead to feelings of loss, low self-esteem, extreme loneliness, and even abandonment. Some adults may experience the "empty nest syndrome," although for most it does not occur. The "empty nesters" tend to be women who have lived vicariously through their children, or men who no longer feel close to their wives and have found their children to be their only source of pleasure. A variation of the "empty nest syndrome" sometimes occurs, which I shall call the "illusive empty nest." This takes place when grown children stay at home too long or return home out of economic necessity, and parents begin to resent this intrusion into what they anticipated as a time to be alone. The full nest seems only to be encouraged by insecure adults, afraid that removing the responsibility for their children will cause them to take responsibility for their own lives. There is no need to discuss the obvious harm visited upon children when dependency is encouraged.

The economic stress of college tuition or medical expenses may take their toll at middle-age. Overwork or job-related problems can add additional stress. Middle-agers may feel the "middle-age squeeze" that results from pressure at the lower age level from teenagers, coupled with pressure from older family members who may begin to have special needs. For this reason, those at mid-life have often been referred to as the "sandwich generation." Women, especially, may feel these pressures since they are usually the most frequent caregivers. Often a loss of personal identity is felt as one is pressed between the demands of the generation below (one's children) and the generation above (one's parents). This may all be going on while the woman is experiencing crises of her own. It is difficult for teenagers who are grappling with identity problems to even take the time to realize that their parents may be going through identity crises as well.

Hope remains strong that each person at middle-age will handle one of these problems in a way that is productive and fulfilling. One woman, who felt that nothing meant anything to her anymore, was lonely and bored and watched television a lot, tried the three Gs—Get up, Get dressed, and Get going.[8] She did just that and is now working; looks forward to each day; and is attractive, interesting, and energetic.

One man, who was a busy manager in a large firm and who loved his work and family, found himself reflecting on his own life after experiencing the death of his best friend. He worked most evenings and weekends and, even though he loved his job, he knew he had to set a better balance in life. By spending more time with his family and resetting his priorities he is now happier than he has ever been.

Another woman, who had never worked before, found herself divorced. She used volunteer work as a first step toward a new career.

A lonely single man, frustrated with his job, changed to a type of work that brought him the opportunity for new friends and the chance to feel needed, wanted, and appreciated.

Then there was the woman who was widowed while still in her forties. She went back to college and liked it so well that she went on for graduate work and obtained a responsible job.

The stories are many, and all do not have happy endings; but what seems to be the best advice at mid-life is to always be willing to accept the challenge of change. It is an inevitable part of life, and by ignoring it we become stagnant. When we react to it we come alive.

NOTES

1. Lynda Madaras and Jane Patterson, *Womancare: A Gynecological Guide to Your Body* (New York: Avon Books, 1981), 608-614.
2. Ibid.
3. Ibid.
4. *Family Circle* magazine (March 19, 1985): 60-64.
5. Edward M. Brecher, *Love, Sex, and Aging: A Consumers Union Report* (Mt. Vernon, N.Y.: Consumers Union, 1984), 287-310.
6. Dierdre Martin, "Batteries Not Included," *The Spectrum*, The State University of New York at Buffalo (February 25, 1983).
7. Gail Sheehy, *Passages* (New York: Bantam Books, 1976), 207-210.
8. Marilyn Lyman, "Feeling Fit in the Forties and Fifties" (Syracuse, N.Y.: Planned Parenthood Center, Inc., 1980), 13.

5

Married Women and Married Men

What to Do When We've Done It All Many Times Before

"Thus we see that the strong man is most secure who has the sympathy of a virtuous, faithful wife, and a frail, timid woman needs the strong arm of manhood upon which to lean. Each needs the other, and God created them in pairs."

Eugenics, 1915

Married couples get bored with each other, not only sexually but emotionally and intellectually. To keep sex alive, it is important to think of new things to do and/or new places to do them. It is likewise important to find new things to think about and with which to be concerned. For couples who wonder if they are open to new ideas, each partner could ask himself or herself the following questions:

1. Even though it may seem improper or shameful, am I willing to think about doing something sexual but different with my spouse?
2. Am I willing to really *do* it?

3. Am I willing to ask my spouse to do it?

If both partners answer no to all three questions, then the couple, neither being willing, should work on other aspects of their lives. If each partner answers yes to two or three of the questions, then they are ready for adventure! In cases where the answers of both partners are not very similar, considerable communication should arise since both sets of desires cannot be satisfied simultaneously. Counseling may prove helpful to both persons.

It is important for couples to realize that their mutual feelings are what count, not what others think. A couple can still be happy sexually if they both agree that intercourse should only occur between married people and only in the "missionary" position. It is when there are disagreements, as to what is "correct" sexual expression that problems arise.

Sexual activity does progressively diminish as couples grow older. Marital intercourse falls from an average frequency of four times per week with couples in their twenties to once a week for those in their sixties. Women and men both report that less frquency is determined more by the man than by the woman. Remember, this generation of elders has allowed the man to call all the shots, not only in family decisions but in the bedroom as well.

Women generally withstand sexual aging better than men, although both experience a decrease in glandular activity. As we found in our discussion of female physiology, the female genitalia do gradually atrophy, but a woman's ability to experience frequent orgasm compensates for this. It is thought that statistics should, in fact, show a greater interest and involvement in sex on the part of women than men, especially if partners were available and if society gave permission for women to express their sexual proclivities.

According to information collected by Elaine Partnow and published in her book *Breaking the Age Barrier,*[1] the majority of couples establish sexual patterns early in their marriage. These patterns change very little after the couple's first year together. Where and when they make love (the time of day and even which days of the week) become habitual and, eventually, monotonous. Even unmarried couples who live together experience the same kind of sexual doldrums.

Men, pushing themselves hard in the professional world, are often too tired for love-making, which, when coupled with a changing physique—protruding belly, flabby midsection—and self-consciousness around grown children, are factors in the spiraling divorce rate. Women, too, who are active in professional life and have major responsibiilty for the house and children, often find themselves too tired for love-making.

Perhaps it would be interesting for those readers who are married to take a short quiz that tests how old their marriage is. This does not measure how many years a couple has been married but how young (immature) versus old (mature) the marriage is. The test, excerpted in part from Partnow's book, results in a "Marital Age Quotient."

Go through the test as thoughtfully and as thoroughly as you can. Do not concern yourself with scoring until you have answered all the questions. Circle the letter assigned to the answer most applicable to you, as per the following example:

1. Do you eat your meals . . .?

   c. at regular hours

   f. irregularly

   e. skip any

   f. nibble throughout the day

   You may note some questions have two "bs" or three "gs" among the choice of answers. Disregard any meaning of the letters at this time. Instructions for scoring are at the end of the test. Here's the scale:

A=5 B=15 C=25 D=35 E=45 F=55 G=65 H=75

At the end of each section write the total number of questions answered for that section on the line indicated thus: NUMBER OF QUESTIONS ANSWERED (6). Divide the sum total of points for each section by the number of questions answered for that section. For example, let's say the sum total of your answers is 150 points and you only answered eight of the nine questions. You would divide 150 by 8, thus your quotient would be 18.75 or, when rounded off, 19. Thus:

TOTAL POINTS: 150

NUMBER OF QUESTIONS ANSWERED: (8)

MARRIAGE QUOTIENT: 18.8 (or about 19)

Marital Age

1. Is your relationship with your mate . . .?

    e. highly satisfactory

    d. somewhat satisfactory

    c. somewhat unsatisfactory

    b. very unsatisfactory

2. Are you having, or have you had, extramarital relationships?

    c. sometimes, but not often

    e. only once or twice

    c. never

    b. pretty frequently

3. Do you and your partner share recreational activities (bowling, hiking, playing cards, etc.)?

    g. once or twice a year

    h. never

    e. several times a year

    d. at least once a month

4. What is your estimate of dependency in your relationship?

    g. we are too independent of one another

    c. my mate is too dependent on me

    a. we are too dependent on one another

b. I am too dependent on my mate

e. our interdependence is well balanced

5. Do you and your mate share important decision-making?

e. frequently

f. only on occasion

g. never or hardly ever

c. always

6. Do you and your mate share private time together?

e. very often

d. occasionally

g. very infrequently

h. never or hardly ever

7. What is your attitude toward achieving an intimate relationship?

e. it is very desirable

g. it is undesirable

h. it is a matter of indifference

8. What actual changes have the passing years made on your relationship?

h. none to speak of

d. it has vastly improved

b. it has deteriorated badly

e. it has acquired a more even keel

9. If you were faced with divorce, which of the following would best apply to you?
   c. if my partner wanted it, I'd grant it
   d. if I were unhappy, I'd demand it
   a. I'd never divorce, no matter what
   b. if I were unhappy, I'd just learn to live with it
   e. whoever wanted it, I'd try anything to save the marriage before divorcing

TOTAL POINTS:

NUMBER OF QUESTIONS ANSWERED: ( )

MARITAL AGE:

My daughter and son-in-law, who have been married six years, took this test and scored 38.3 years. I would say that is a very mature marriage in number of years for so few years of actual marriage. How did you do?

Nearly 95 percent of Americans marry at some time in their lives, but many of these marriages result in divorce or in widowhood. Most of those who lose their spouses are women. The average marriage lasts 6.5 years. Median age at the time of a person's first divorce is about 30 for men, 28 for women. Many marriages end within the first two years. More than half the people who get divorced remarry, and most of them marry someone who has also been married before. For second marriages, the average age for men is 39.9 for women 36.5.[2]

Marriages that last beyond the parenting years often experience a second honeymoon. Historically, this period of married life is relatively new since it was rare for both parents to live beyond the time the last child left the nest. Today, men are about fifty-four and women about fifty-one when their last child leaves home.

Parenthood is hard on love relationships. The first years after a baby is born result in a noticeable drop in marital satisfaction. The level of satisfaction never reaches the euphoric levels with which it began until the last child leaves home. Most couples find this new time for being alone a great pleasure. Raising a family apparently was not as much fun to do as it is to be done with.[3]

What are happy love relationships like in later life? What is valued most? As a group, older lovers value emotional security above all: being able to depend and trust one another. Also valued are respect and admiration. A third important dimension is the ability to communicate and be honest with each other. A sixty-two-year-old man said, "I share my joys, sorrows, and adventures with her and she does the same with me, giving us twice as much fun as we would have individually."

A fourth dimension is spending time together, working and playing. A fifth dimension of love is sexual intimacy. One sixty-year-old put it this way: "She is physically pleasing to all my senses—different at different times of life, but always pleasing."

A final dimension is loyalty. For one older mother of three, what makes her relationship satisfying is that, "He acts as though he expects to spend the rest of his life with me."[4]

One question immediately comes to mind. Are these the same characteristics valued at any age? When I asked college students how they felt about love I received such answers as:

> "Love is when two people are committed enough to each other to form a partnership despite their differences and because of their similarities."

> "Love is a commitment. It is a commitment that leads to the growth of each person in the relationship. Love is a journey in getting to know another person, ultimately. It is an ongoing experience with ups and downs, joys and sorrows, but through it all you know your life has been mutually enriched."

> "It's hard to define love because it's a *life long process*. It depends on your age, relationships, what you look for in a person. Right now love is communication—talking with each other honestly, a continuous learning experience, i.e., learning other points of view, feelings, sexually sharing a deep experience with one another. Love is growing with each other."

Most older married couples describe their long-lasting marriages as very much like they were early on, yet different in very special ways.

The nature of love changes as needs change. Certainly the love from our parents is different from that of a mate, yet in some ways the same. Likewise, through all the years of marriage, developmental changes occur that can affect and vary the needs of love between husband and wife. The nature of a new love is certainly different from the nature of a love that has been shared for fifty years.

Couples who describe changes in their relationship over the years note that the relationship becomes closer and deeper, having experienced the ups and downs of life together, the good times and the bad. One retired school teacher described the change in love by saying, "Our love has deepened, our understanding of each other has grown. Our life experiences together have drawn us closer together." Some older lovers describe a greater sense of affection and understanding that makes the relationship closer. One man described his fifty-four-year love relationship in this way: "It has changed from exciting, romantic thrills to comfortable, warm, happy affection. Our vigor has certainly lessened. Our problems are fewer and different. We have switched from making and caring for babies to caring for doctors, politicians, and tax collectors."

Another change in relationships over time is the presence of more patience, acceptance, and tolerance for one's partner. Young adults seem to struggle to cope with each other's strengths and weaknesses. Older adults simply accept one another.

A mellowing occurs over a satisfying relationship that has endured over many years, accompanied by more tenderness, affection, and warmth. One man described his forty-year marriage by saying, "Our relationship has improved with age. It has warmed and mellowed. At one time an important element of our relationship, although never the most important element, was the marvelous sexual satisfaction that we enjoyed with considerable frequency. As we have grown older, this aspect has assumed less importance, to be replaced to some extent by less exciting manifestations of our love and affection, such as frequent touching, holding, hugging, kissing, and, of course, continual verbal expressions of love. We feel that at this time we are as much in love, if not more so, than we ever were, as we have a chance to thoroughly enjoy each other exclusively now that our children are grown and have 'left the fold.'"

Sexuality for older couples, in addition to the immediate pleasure of physical intimacy, becomes an affirmation of a lifetime of shared experiences and memories. What makes it last? Older couples have to care enough over the years to listen, to talk honestly to each other when difficulties arise, and to be very patient with one another.

Commitment is necessary, an expectation that the relationship will last. As one man said: "I would rather be with her than anyone else." Another man put it this way: "It's been the best. It still is. What more can I say?"[5]

Many couples have trouble communicating about sex. Those who did not talk about sex in their early years of marriage are probably not communicating now that they have reached their later years. It may be more difficult but never too late to begin communicating. Here are some of the barriers that need to be overcome:[6]

1. *Fear of embarrassment—*

   "I just can't talk about what arouses me most. I wasn't brought up that way."

   "She makes so many distracting remarks. I know I should tell her, but I can't hurt her feelings."

2. *Fear that spontaneity will be ruined—*

   "I feel we're making love by the trial and error system, but I'm afraid I will sound like I'm issuing instructions."

3. *Fear that one's partner will feel threatened—*

   "I'm afraid to say something that might be taken as criticism; but if I say nothing, I know that our sex life will be less satisfying."

4. *Fear of being considered selfish—*

   "I just tell him that's enough because I'm afraid he's getting tired, when I know it just takes more time for me to become aroused than it does him."

Some suggestions to break down these barriers are:[7]

1. Don't hold back your feelings.
2. Create an atmosphere in which both of you feel secure enough to speak freely.
3. Know each other's sexual expectations.
4. Don't expect your partner to read your mind.
5. Use "I" statements: "I'd love for you to rub my back," rather than, "You never rub my back."
6. Use open-ended questions to avoid yes or no answers: "What else would feel good?" rather than, "Does this feel good?"
7. Let your partner know you're just as concerned about his/her sexual needs as you are about your own.
8. Avoid countercomplaining: "I do what you want, but you never do what I want."
9. Be specific. Just asking someone to "be more romantic" doesn't really tell him or her what you want.
10. Think carefully before being totally frank.

Some added suggestions would be to share books, view films together, attend lectures, take part in marriage workshops or seminars, and be willing to seek the help of a marriage counselor or sex therapist if you feel you need a little extra help.

Carol Botwin, in her book *Is There Sex After Marriage?* compiled a list of twenty-three time-tested tips from the experts. The following are offered in the hope of making sex better than ever for any married couple. I have appended comments specifically designed for the older married couple:[8]

1. Evaluate your love life.

   (Not while you're having sex, but during a non-sex time. Can't you just see someone stopping just before an orgasm to say, "Are we really enjoying ourselves?")

2. Make time for sex.

   (After retirement this is not as much of a problem. In some cases, the couple may need to adjust to having *too much* time.)

3. Continue to court each other.

   (Happy long-term relationships are evidenced by a light in each other's eyes when the partner walks into the room.)

4. Don't be afraid to talk about sex.

   (Put aside that stodgy Victorian influence, which has for decades found older people saying, "Us old folks shouldn't talk about such things!")

5. Give positive feedback.

   (Let him or her know that something feels good.)

6. Never fake orgasms.

   (Over time this can lead to the assumption that what is being done is just fine. You can cheat each other out of sexual pleasure.)

7. Use positive reinforcement.

   (Maybe there is an annoying habit [like wearing curlers to bed] that turns you off. Rather than complaining each time, try saying something positive when those curlers are *not* worn to bed.)

8. Tune in to your own sexuality.

   (Did you ever try keeping a sexual journal of what turns you on? What thoughts, feelings, or fantasies? What music?

9. Remember that our sexual selves are part of our entire selves.

   (Older couples, especially women, may never have felt comfortable with their sexual selves. The greater openness with which sex is being treated nowadays seems to help some older women toward discovering their "hidden" self.)

10. Don't be afraid to say no.

    (Being told no is not so much a problem for the younger male, but the older male may feel rejected when "excuses" are given. The woman, who traditionally felt it was an obligation to have sex whenever her husband wanted it, unless she could come up with a good enough "excuse," runs out of excuses over the years. What is needed is a willingness to admit honestly that you don't really feel like making love. A pact needs to be made between a couple beforehand, so that it is understood that this is all right and thus each person respects the right of the other to feel this way.)

11. Recognize the dangers in sexual signals.

    (Saying "I'm going to bed early," meaning "Let's have sex," or "I'm staying up late," meaning "Forget it," can be a negotiation that, as we get older, becomes more tiring. This kind of negotiation may be one reason more older adults are saying, "Well, maybe tomorrow.")

12. Respect each other's tastes.

    (Maybe he likes a certain perfume, but not another. Use it. Maybe she can't stand your after shave. Change it.)

13. Create privacy.

    (Put a lock on the bedroom door when children are still at home. Then thoroughly enjoy the freedom when they're not at home and you don't have to use it.)

14. Guard against rigid routines.

    (Although some people thrive on routine, most find it boring. Change the place, the time, the day, the position, and plan vacations. Even a day or two away revitalizes.)

15. Remember that sex is a way of expressing love.

    (Whether through intercourse or cuddling, sex is more than a physical release in caring relationships.)

16. Use your fantasies.

    (Act out some mutual fantasies and remember that it's perfectly okay to have someone other than your partner starring in your fantasy. That's nothing to feel guilty about, and it can be your own secret.)

17. Take responsibility for your own pleasure.

    (Older women need to work on this, since they learned to expect the man to take charge. It can be a real turn on for a man to feel that the woman has initiated the action.)

18. Don't turn yourself off.

    (Negative thoughts about a partner can, in a split second, take over one's desire and significantly reduce sexual enjoyment. Sex drive is really in the mind. Keep these thoughts from surfacing; think of positive qualities; and concentrate on the pleasure itself.)

19. Don't expect sex to be great all the time.

    (Older couples who have remained together know this to be true, just as they have learned not to expect all of life to be great all the time.)

20. Avoid turning sex into work.

    (I remember being shown through a friend's house and, when approaching the bedroom, being told, "Well, here's the workbench." Don't make sex into work by worrying about your performance.)

21. Remember that the foundation of good sex is respect and trust.

    (Happy older couples have learned that respect means treating each other as equals, and trust means knowing that your partner considers your best interests as well as his or her own.)

22. Don't neglect a sexual problem.

    (You see a doctor for other problems, why not be willing to seek help at any age or at any stage of a relationship? There are competent professionals available if you and/or your partner have not been able to work through a problem yourselves.)

23. Pay special attention to sex as you grow older.

    (Continue to talk to each other about your sexual needs and how you might accommodate one another as new needs arise. If you haven't been talking about sex, it's never too late to start. Fully believe that sex does not end with old age and that you and your partner can continue to give each other pleasure for the rest of your lives.)

In *Love, Sex, and Aging,* Edward Brecher reported the results of his survey of 3,040 wives and husbands (ranging in age from fifty to ninety-three). The data is limited by the fact that it is based only on those who responded to the survey and not those who may be so sexually inhibited that they wouldn't think of answering questions about their sex lives. Nevertheless, it sheds some interesting light on the subject of older married people.

The results showed that 87 percent were happily married and just 13 percent considered themselves unhappily married. One wife of thirty-eight years wrote, "Sometimes I'm so happy I get scared it will cease too soon." An unhappily married wife wrote, "We are in our early fifties and it scares me to think that this is the way it will be the rest of my life. We have two children still at home. . . . I don't know what we will do when they are gone, too."[9]

Brecher reviewed fifteen nonsexual factors and found only one that was closely associated with marital happiness. You may be able to guess what it is. If you said "communication," you were right. The quality of communication makes an important contribution to the degree of marital happiness.

When asked how important the sexual side of marriage is, more husbands (87 percent) than wives (25 percent) thought it was very or moderately important. Twenty-five percent of the wives and 12 percent of the husbands thought it was of little importance.

A sixty-five-year-old husband, married for thirty-nine yers, commented: "I was surprised that our sex life kept on being enjoyable. I thought when I was younger that by my age it would all be over.

[Sex is] less intense and less frequent [now], but very enjoyable and satisfying."[10]

In contrast, one fifty-nine-year-old wife, married thirty-six years, reported: "Sex was never a big deal anyway, but I enjoyed it once things were started. Now I want to get it over with as quickly as possible."

Couples who still have intercourse report happier marriages (91 percent) than those who do not (69 percent). Of those having intercourse, 76 percent of wives and 87 percent of husbands rated their enjoyment of sex as high. Both wives and husbands who reported high enjoyment of sex also reported a high proportion of happy marriages. Satisfaction, however, is less closely linked to frequency of sex.

The proportion of unhappily married wives is exceedingly high among those who want less sex. Most wives (77 percent) feel the frequency of sex is just right but only 59 percent of husbands agree. When one partner wants sex more frequently than another, difficulties may arise. A sixty-two-year-old wife says that she and her husband have sex about once a week and this is too frequent for her. The husband says they have sex two or three times a week and this is not frequent enough for him.

According to Brecher's study, the popular idea that orgasm is important for the husbands but not the wives simply does not hold true. Both wives and husbands who, at least usually, achieve orgasm are more likely to report happy marriages.[11]

Communication about sex, just like communication in general, is associated with happy marriages. A sixty-eight-year-old wife, married for fifty-two years, wrote that her husband tried to initiate discussions of sex but she resisted. Then, she continued, "I finally took time to read a book and discovered what my husband *tried* to tell me was true." They are now comfortable about sex. Many responded about the impact that lack of communication has had on their marital relations.

As far as interest in sex is concerned, the amount of interest on the part of the husbands does not seem to have an effect on their attitudes about being happily married. One in four women, though, whose interest in sex is weak or absent, reports unhappiness in marriage. The results are approximately the same for ease of sexual arousal. Questions pertaining to who initiates sexual activity still elicit responses that reflect the attitudes of a generation brought up during a time when males took the lead in everything. However, in marriages where the lead was equally shared, there was a greater degree of marital satisfaction.

Brecher's interview included extramarital relationships. He found that for most adulterous wives, sex outside marriage seemed to be a serious, significant experience, whereas men considered it a more casual matter. Most wives and husbands considered fidelity important. The double standard of adulterous husbands with faithful wives still outnumbered adulterous wives with faithful husbands. Consensual adultery for both partners was seen infrequently. Eighty-seven percent of faithful wives and 91 percent of faithful husbands rated their marriages as happy. But a substantial number of adulterous wives (72 percent) and husbands (75 percent) also rated their marriages as happy.[12]

The *Starr-Weiner Report on Sex and Sexuality in the Mature Years,* produced by Bernard D. Starr and Marcella Bakur Weiner, also focuses on a survey of adults over age sixty. The survey uses open-ended questions and was given after talks by the researchers at community centers and other facilities frequented by older adults. There were 800 respondents. When asked if they liked sex, a resounding 97 percent in the 60-69 and 70-79 age groups said yes. Ninety-three percent of those in the 80-91 age group responded positively.

Some interesting comments were made by those married adults in the study who, when asked, said they liked sex:[13]

(Male, age 65): "Yes. Doesn't everyone?"

(Male, age 68): "Yes. Like everything about it."

(Female, age 72): "Yes. I believe it relieves the pressures of life. I feel much better physically and mentally when enjoying a good sex life."

(Female, age 65): "Yes. It is a natural way to ease the loneliness inherent in being an individual. It feels good, and now I learned it's good for easing arthritis."

(Male, age 80): "Yes. I like sex because it's a feeling you do not forget."

(Male, age 63): "I have throughout my life been thrilled by the feel of a female body and still feel the same."

(Female, age 63): "Yes. Why not? Am I different now from when I was younger? Only my outer shell has changed."

(Male, age 69): "Yes. Sex is one of the pleasures of life. It is also one way in which men and women overcome loneliness and frustration. There's the added pleasure that, as we grow older, we can still enjoy sex and thus still to be counted as total men and women.

(Male, age 67): "Very much. I love the fondling, touching, nakedness, and all the methods of achieving the end result."

(Female, age 64): "Yes, with all my heart. I don't know how to explain except it is beautiful to me."

(Female, age 66): "Yes—it makes me feel young."

(Female, age 63): "Yes—and it helps to mitigate our sense of aloneness."

(Male, age 83): "Yes. It's a pleasure."

(Male, age 75): "To me sex can be beautiful if there is no guilt involved by either one; if they let themselves go."

Several years ago "Dear Abby" took a Sex Survey. It was inspired by a letter from a reader who signed herself "Tired in Lincoln, Nebraska." She wrote that at age fifty, after thirty years of marriage, she was tired of sex. "I can't believe I'm the only woman who feels this way," she wrote. "Please poll your readers, Abby, and if they're honest, I think you'll find I'm right."

Abby received 106,448 responses, an amazing number. Of these, 61,055 agreed with TIRED and 45,393 disagreed. Here are some sample comments:

> "I am 50, raised two children, married 29 years, cared for a semi-invalid mother, moved 14 times, worked almost my entire married life as a nurse, and believe it or not, it's my HUSBAND who's tired! . . . Richmond, Va."

"I always took a couple of stiff drinks to face what was waiting for me in the bedroom. I'm 63, and still hate sex, but I sure love booze. . . . Baltimore, Md."

"There must be something wrong with TIRED. I'm 81, and when my husband was alive I thought sex was the most fun in the world, but now that I'm a widow, it's kind of hard to find someone to play with—especially in a small town where everyone knows your business. . . . Having Fun at 81."

"I'm 51, and now that our kids are out of the house we can make love in the afternoon, make all the noise we want, and I don't have to worry about getting pregnant. This is the best time of my life! . . . Happy in Denver."

"How can I enjoy sex when my husband comes to bed with his teeth out, needing a bath, and belching onions in my face? I'm 55 and agree with TIRED . . . no name in Cleveland."

"I'm pushing 85, and hope that the last healthy breath God gives me will be spent in an intimate embrace with my man . . . M. in San Diego."

"I'm glad for a chance to express my feelings. I agree with TIRED. My husband is 62, a severe arthritic, and he's NEVER tired. He claims that sex is beneficial to his health. The only place he doesn't have arthritis is you-know-where. Don't use my name. I am 58 and have felt this way for the last 20 years . . . A in Syracuse."

"At 50 I got nothing out of sex. I thought I was frigid, but something happened somewhere around 53, and now we're more compatible sexually than we've ever been. Hard work and money worries make a man a poor lover . . . N.Y.C."

"I've been a widow for 12 years. My husband and I both enjoyed sex until he died. He was 90. I could still enjoy it, but who would have me? . . . JUNE, age 81."

"I was told that a decent woman wasn't supposed to enjoy sex, so I felt guilty when I did. My husband died, and when I married again at 46, I learned how to enjoy sex without shame or guilt. Sex with the right man is wonderful . . . Laura, age 77."[14]

As one can see from the above comments, there are varying opinions about sex over the years. One thing they seem to have in common, though, is strength of conviction!

Perhaps this chapter can best be summarized by a wonderful quotation from Alex Comfort, who can be counted among the older generation himself. He wrote the following in his book, *The Joy of Sex:*

> The only thing age has to do with sex performance is that the longer you love, the more you learn. Young people (and some older ones) are firmly convinced that no one over fifty makes love, and it would be pretty obscene if they did. Ours isn't the first generation to know otherwise, but probably the first one which hasn't been brainwashed into being ashamed to admit it![15]

NOTES

1. Elaine Partnow, *Breaking the Age Barrier* (New York: Pinnacle Books, 1981). Material cited in *Los Angeles Times* syndicated story.
2. Ibid.
3. Margaret Neiswender Reedy, "What Happens to Love?: Love, Sexuality and Aging," in *Sexuality and Aging,* Robert Solnick (ed.) (Los Angeles: The University of Southern California Press, 1978), 184-95.
4. Ibid.
5. Ibid.
6. Norman Lobsenz, "The Gentle Art of Talking About Sex," in *Human Sexuality,* annual editions, edited by Ollie Pocs (Guilford, Conn.: Dushkin Publishing Group, 1986), 145-46.
7. Ibid.
8. Carl Botwin, *Is There Sex After Marriage?* (Boston: Little, Brown and Co., 1985), 247-65.
9. Edward M. Brecher, *Love, Sex, and Aging: A Consumers Union Report* (Mt. Vernon, N.Y.: Consumers Union, 1984), 48.
10. Ibid., 84-85.
11. Ibid., 93.
12. Ibid., 140-141.
13. Bernard D. Starr and Marcella Bakur Weiner, *The Starr-Weiner Report on Sex and Sexuality in the Mature Years* (New York: McGraw Hill, 1981), 36-38.
14. Abigail Van Buren, "Dear Abby: Sex Survey Continues," pub-

lished by the United Press Syndicate and reprinted in *The Courier Express* (Buffalo, New York).

15. Alex Comfort, *The Joy of Sex* (New York: Crown Publishers, 1972), 224.

6

Unmarried Women and Unmarried Men

Finding Each Other or Going It Alone

"Single life is forced upon many of both sexes because of peculiar conditions and circumstances, but theirs is not the ideal life. There is in store for such as these who are not permitted to enjoy the fruits of love a hope for the future which enables them to bear with fortitude the present."

Eugenics, 1915

Chapter 5 ended with a quote from Alex Comfort, and the present chapter will begin with one. I'll explain why as soon as we've had an opportunity to appreciate what he has to say.

> The best producer of an active and pleasurable sex life in the later years is an active and pleasurable sex life in the early years; the things that stop a person from having sex with increasing age are exactly the things that stop one from bicycle riding: bad health, thinking it looks silly, not having a bicycle. The difference is they happen later for sex than for bicycles.

This chapter is going to talk about bicycles and those who don't have them. First we'll talk about who is most likely not to have a bicycle; how this affects their sex lives; and, finally, what can be done about it. This discussion should have special meaning for our bicycleless population and for their families, who need to understand the adjustment of a parent who no longer has a partner. Also mentioned will be single people who never had a bicycle of their own and divorced people who have traded theirs in for a different model or are still shopping around.

Who are most likely not to have a bicycle? Women! The "weaker" sex survives, the "stronger" sex does not. From the very beginning, more boy babies are conceived than girl babies, but more die in the womb. At birth, there are more boy babies born than girl babies, but more succumb to the birth trauma. More boys than girls die of infectious diseases and accidents in childhood. During adolescence the trend continues, aided by suicide and homicide. By young adulthood, enough men have died that a leveling effect occurs and there are now as many women as men. This, however, is only momentary, for men continue to die at greater rates than women until, by old age, there exists an imbalance of such proportions that it seems all old people are women.

Have you ever noticed a group of senior citizens in a restaurant? It reminds me of my field trip days with fifth graders when, as their teacher, I led the way. So, too, it seems that the one or two conspicuous men in this large congregation of older people must surely be leading the way. If not leading the way, they are, at the very least, the centers of attention: fussed over, sought after, and deferred to.

Observe what happens when a single man moves into a retirement complex. One friend of mine, an older gentleman, confided that he had to hide the cakes, pies, and cookies that arrived at his door so as not to offend the next bearer of goodies. The same type of attention can be observed at a senior citizen center where a single man is invited, encouraged, and sometimes even begged to take part in every activity available, except maybe sewing. Witness dinner time at a nursing home, where the few able men are faced with the dilemma of which chair, of the many saved for them, they should sit at.

Older men become the leaders of this large army of older women, based not upon ability, but upon gender. Just as it is in the predominantly female fields of teaching and nursing, where the few men available receive the promotions whether as qualified as the women or not, so, too, this prejudice exists in the female dominated world (in numbers only) of older people. Certainly there are exceptions, especially as those new to the older generation move up and begin to reflect a society in which women are beginning, albeit slowly, to be placed in positions of leadership. However, it must be remembered that we are talking about bicycles and sex, and older women learned to ride with men doing the steering.

Female longevity, then, is a considerable barrier to sexual activity for older women. Not only do women live on the average seven years longer than men, but they are approximately three years younger than the men they marry. This means that the average woman can expect to spend approximately ten years as a widow.

The obvious way to prevent this is for women to marry men approximately eight years younger than themselves to make up for the difference in life expectancy. Perhaps we are seeing a slight trend here, but very slight. A few years ago the difference in age of men and women at the time of marriage was four years rather than the three now reported.

Besides enjoying the greater possibility of having a partner in old age if married to someone eight years younger than herself, a woman also has the additional advantage of greater sexual compatibility. The reason for this is that men reach their sexual peak at a younger age than women. With this data in mind, it would be better for a woman to marry someone even younger than the suggested eight years. This difference in sexual interest and capacity is not biologically defined but rather is the result of social conditioning. The old double standard that says it's all right for boys to be sexually active but not girls is alive and well. Think of your own sexual upbringing. Aren't siblings given the message that having sex is all right and perfectly "natural" for one's brother but not all right and definitely promiscuous for one's sister?

If a woman marries someone younger, she risks being the object of society's catcalls rather than its applause. The younger man, too, will be looked upon as somewhat peculiar for desiring an older woman. Occasionally, though, there are the "Mrs. Robinsons" who enter into teacher relationships with younger men. This doesn't happen for the older man-younger woman liaison. Such relationships are often the victims of our society's picture of the older woman as wrinkled and ugly, and the older man as wrinkled and distinguished. Power comes into play here as well; it is not appropriate somehow for a man—the powerful one—to put himself in the position of being dominated by an older woman. Actress Hermione Gingold, who died recently, talked about her romance with a younger man. Finally, after sixteen years, she agreed to become engaged but would not marry him. He was thirty-three and she was seventy-four at the time. She was firm in her belief that all this talk of age is disgusting and that women's liberation should come in on it and set things straight. (See the Appendix for Benjamin Franklin's eight reasons for marrying an older woman.)

In the *Starr-Weiner Report*, just less than four percent of the total sample suggested a younger man as a viable option for older women. A married male, age sixty-nine, suggested that it might be necessary for a woman to pay for the services of a younger man.[2] The small percentage of older people suggesting older woman-younger man liaisons is indicative of how unlikely it is to actually happen. Society tends to control this. What would you do or say if your mother introduced you to a considerably younger man as her friend and you began to realize that there was more than friendship involved? It is at this moment easy to intellectualize about what you might say, but as you continue on in this and remaining chapters, it is more important to visualize the situation actually happening in your own family. One of the easiest things we do in life is judge what is happening to others. One of our most difficult tasks is looking fairly at what is happening to ourselves and to those we love so dearly.

Imagine your next door neighbor has just told you that her Aunt Jane, age sixty-eight, is marrying someone age forty. Intellectually you may say, "Good for her!" or "Why not? Whatever makes her happy!" Now imagine, instead, that it is your own mother who is marrying someone age forty, someone your very own age. Emotions run rampant over any efforts to intellectualize and it is difficult, if possible, to say, "Good for her!" "Why not? Whatever makes her happy!" Some people will eventually be able to accept this, though not as easily when it is their own mother. Others may never be able to react in a positive way. It's the old "I'll-accept-anything-as-long-as-it-doesn't-affect-me-or-threaten-my-values" syndrome.

Interestingly, this same study (Starr-Weiner) does indicate a strong acceptance among the older population for an older woman-younger man combination. Eighty-three percent voiced enthusiastic support, compared to just three percent more (86 percent) for an older man-younger woman combination.[3] Why, then, is this not reflected in the actual forming of such relationships? Is it possible that the respondents are giving what they feel to be the "right" answers but could not really act upon the idea themselves? It may be an indication, though, of a future trend. Although it may not be happening often, perhaps the stage is being set for future "performances."

Age is certainly one factor in predicting the compatibility of two persons. It does affect our ability to place individuals into generations whose history, values, and shared events influence personal behavior. However, it is only one of several factors that bear upon a relationship. If similarity of interests is combined with a true sense of personal identity that allows for the development of self while encouraging true caring, then an age difference, no matter how great, becomes inconsequential. For the two individuals who have traded personal loneliness for a togetherness born of companionship, mutual love, and respect, their personal fulfillment could be purchased at the cost of social ostracism. Since our friends are usually people close to our own age, where does this couple fit in? Who will accept them into their social group? No matter how much they love each other, it takes added strength to face the rejection of others. This is most especially noticeable when the woman is the older of the two. So, in effect, it is a trade off: the older woman trades personal loneliness for social loneliness.

Edward Brecher, in his Consumers Union Report on *Love, Sex, and Aging,* reports on some of these women, most of whom consider the trade off to be positive. A fifty-year-old woman comments, "I really feel at this point in my life that age is about 80 percent mental and 20 percent physical. I have seen and known people in their late 20s who are old simply because they are bored with life, have closed their minds to all the exciting possibilities out there."[4] One woman, age fifty-four, embarked upon a love affair with a man of thirty-five whom she had known for many years. They have sex once a day or more and report high levels of satisfaction on the life enjoyment scale. However, she identifies communication as only "good," explaining that the age difference leaves so much that can't be shared.[5]

Since great numbers of older women are not experiencing relationships with younger men, what are the alternatives? One is abstinence (remaining celibate), diverting the energy usually spent on sexual pursuits into such activities as church work, the business world, volunteer and social work. Some women might become overzealous in mothering their maturing children or grandchildren. They may exhaust themselves physically in frantic attempts, whether conscious or unconscious, to relieve the accumulated sexual tensions that are often unrecognized. Occasionally, this may turn into an obsessional neurosis, such as the sixty-three-year-old woman who, following the death of her husband, exhibited a hand-washing compulsion that, for many years, was undiagnosed as the result of the lack of a sexual outlet.

Friendship is an obvious solution to the problem of loneliness, but it may not provide the sexual release that a woman has come to expect. Friendships and close relatives, however, can provide the caring and warmth that help us identify ourselves as sexual beings. Of special importance may be the generative element emerging through intergenerational relationships: the old with the young, whether one's own children and grandchildren or someone else's. The theorist Erik Erikson identifies the stage of generativity versus despair, in which the older person receives great satisfaction from passing on his or her knowledge and wisdom to younger generations, whether as a mentor or as a good friend. Again, however, although love may be a part of this, it does not provide for a release from sexual tension. This leads us to the next alternative, the development of a homosexual relationship between women who had previously identified themselves as heterosexual.

This alternative may generate tremendous guilt for older women. However, consider the comments of a fifty-four-year-old woman who wrote that she had never had a sexual relationship with another woman, but has been sexually attracted to other women both before and after the age of fifty. She writes: "I believe I am, and all people are, potentially bisexual. Pleasure is pleasure, and given the appropriate cultural and personal stimulus, how can the genitals tell the difference?"[6]

Touching can lead to an orgasm, whether the result of being touched by the opposite sex, the same sex, or oneself. If a woman has no one else to touch her but another woman, might this not lead to an orgasm? Can you accept this? Is this, then, homosexuality? Or is it the result, instead, of two people who care about each other, not really desiring each other sexually, but providing the ultimate in caring by bringing each other pleasure in the form of a sexual release? Is it possible for a daughter or son to take the attitude that this is all right for a parent?

Actually, it may be more likely that present and future generations will accept this than it is for our current elder population. The future generation of elder women will have experienced in their early years an increasing openness about sexual practices. Rather than accepting what life has dealt them, in being one of the many women alone versus their married sisters, they have learned to be women who take charge of their own lives. This includes making their own decisions about abandoning sexuality. There is no reason to expect that this need they have to control their own lives will change as they get older.

As a result of this and the greater openness toward homosexuality (especially lesbianism, since it is not affected by AIDS), coupled with a growing number of women who report homosexual experiences at some time in their lives, it is easy to speculate that the homosexual alternative will become more viable as heterosexual relationships narrow. It may be just for the release that an orgasm brings, or it may be based upon a true love and affection that our Western society has always looked upon as a necessary and idealized part of any sexual relationship.

If, in fact, we accept the well-known writings of psychologists like Carl Jung, we must accept that there is a masculine and feminine component in each of us. One component becomes dominant and guides our sexual identity, while societal pressures offer reinforcement and confirmation. However, it is well documented that in cases of isolation, such as that experienced in prisons, our other side may emerge. This, too, can relate to the isolation of old age and to the decision by women to find alternatives rather than accept alienation. It has even been suggested that "younger women may opt for the bisexual choice sooner as a means of preparing for the future."[7]

Another option is masturbation. This does not help as much with our psychological self as it does with our physical self, but there still is something to be said for enjoying and reveling in one's own body.

Attitudes toward masturbation have been a detriment to its use as a form of relief from sexual tension, especially for older women. Masturbation needs to be stressed as an acceptable alternative for those women who cannot find a suitable sexual partner. Self-stimulation can be very important in providing a regular and satisfying release of sexual tension. It can also help keep the sexual "apparatus" running smoothly (the use it or lose it idea), in case one does find a suitable partner. Yet many older women still have irrational reservations about masturbation. Consider the attitudes with which they were confronted when young girls: masturbation was called "self-abuse" and thought to cause insanity, early decrepitude, permanent nervous afflictions, blindness, mental impairment, loss of memory, hemorrhaging, falling of the womb, cancer, cardiac disorders, spinal problems, palpitations, hysteria, convulsions, and emaciation. Men, too, were not exempt from the masturbation taboo. It certainly was easy in those days to prevent a wide variety of conditions. All that was necessary, apparently, was to refrain from self-stimulation and a long, healthy life, was yours! It was easy to see that masturbation caused insanity, wasn't it? Think of all the masturbatory activity observed in insane asylums.

Many women were taught to feel that it was improper to touch their genitals, even when bathing. Mary, a client of mine, remembered being "caught" by her grandmother while washing "down there" and was admonished never to do that again. Her grandmother told her that only bad little girls touch themselves there. In this case, I advised using a device such as a vibrator, or even an electric toothbrush, until she felt comfortable using her own hands. Many people are surprised to find that over 80 percent of women masturbate regularly or have at some time. Few are surprised to know that over 90 percent of men do. Masturbation has always been considered more of a male activity. Many people are also surprised to know that a large number of men and women who have partners continue to masturbate, and a good number engage in mutual masturbation.

For men, bicycles are more available in that those who find themselves without a partner have a large "selection" to choose from. Newer models are available, as well as many worn and reconditioned ones. The opportunities are plentiful and the majority of single men waste little time in finding another model.

Although far fewer men live alone, single males are not as well adjusted as single females. Therefore, being alone is more of a problem for them. Various studies of life satisfaction among married and unmarried people generally point to higher levels of happiness for married men. Next are single women, followed by married women, with single men trailing last. It is generally felt that the difference in life satisfaction between single women and single men is affected by the social support mechanisms women have access to, especially the strong emotional ties with friends, unlike the "locker room" (less well bonded) friendships more typical of men.

Most older men live with their wives, whereas most older women live alone. The statistics are glaring. For those individuals age seventy-five and older, two-thirds of the men live with a spouse while only one-fifth of the women do. Remarriage becomes a male prerogative. After age sixty-five, men are eight times more likely to remarry than are women. The less a man has in resources, such as education and income, the more likely he is to remarry; while for a woman the more resources she has, the less likely she is to remarry.[8] As stated previously, the fact that men are scarce in later life and tend to marry younger women adds to a definite imbalance in remarriage opportunities, depending on whether one is male or female.

Remarriage in later life is sometimes more of an adjustment for the family than it is for the two individuals involved, who simply need to get used to riding a tandem bicycle again. It is sometimes felt that a second marriage may repeat the problems of the first. Most older couples do report happiness in their second marriages. The best advice for older people who are considering marriage is the same offered to younger people: wait for at least two years before deciding to marry. This allows for the romance of the moment to lose some of its novelty, at least enough so that both people can take a look at what is left after the excitement of sex has calmed. Yes, the sexual attraction is as much a part of the relationship for an older couple as it is for two younger people. After falling "in love," the couple must fall "out of love" for a period of time, during which they can step back from the situation and more realistically look at all other aspects of the relationship. As with younger couples, the chances for a happier marriage increase when this is done.

A small percentage of our elders have never married. A very small percentage of them will marry after age fifty. For the most part, those who have remained single (especially women), report few negative effects, though the adjustment to marriage may, in effect, be difficult for those who have remained single for many years.

If there were equal numbers of men and women in later years, most experts agree that women would be the more active sex. A woman's sex drive continues to grow until age thirty and then levels off throughout the remainder of her life. A man's sex drive peaks early, and progressively lessens; for some, it disappears altogether in advanced age.

This chapter has explored the world of single persons, a world in which we will all live for some period of our lives. It is becoming more and more populated as an increasing divorce rate, when added to mortality figures, results in greater probability of more people spending years alone. How these years are managed by each of us is determined not only by environmental constraints but also by our own initiative in overcoming sexual barriers.

Perhaps the best advice is to do your own bicycle shopping and leave well-meaning family and friends waiting outside the shop. After all, the older you are the more you know your own likes and dislikes. There are many colors, sizes, and speeds. The choice should be yours.

NOTES

1. Alex Comfort, *The Joy of Sex* (New York: Crown Publishers, 1972), 220.
2. Bernard D. Starr and Marcela Bakur-Weiner, *The Starr-Weiner Report on Sex and Sexuality in the Mature Years* (New York: McGraw Hill, 1981), 172.
3. Ibid., 173.
4. Edward M. Brecher, *Love, Sex and Aging: A Consumers Union Report* (Mt. Vernon, New York: Consumers Union, 1984), 188.
5. Ibid., 190.
6. Ibid.
7. Starr and Bakur-Weiner, op. cit., 249.

8. Jack C. Horn and Jeff Meer, "The Vintage Years," *Psychology Today* (May 1987): 84.

7

Homosexual Relationships

The Forgotten Older Minority

"All men are made to love and be loved. The manifestations, or expressions, of love are called forth by a variety of agencies. There is Christian love. It is a form of love belonging to the Christian life. At the time of conversion and as one develops in the Christian life, he has an unselfish love for both sexes, all ages, all races, rich and poor that does not belong to the unconverted life. This love grows out of a changed moral relation to man and God."

Eugenics, 1915

Older persons are often stereotyped, but add to this the predominantly negative social attitudes toward homosexuals and it is not at all difficult to see how the combination of being old and gay may present a unique problem. Older gay men have been repeatedly singled out by younger gays as particularly pathetic figures. The myths that younger homosexuals perpetuate regarding the "old queens" contain no more fact than myths about elders in general. Older homosexuals face the same problems encountered by many older persons, but the aging homosexual is thought to become more distinctly odd as he or she ages. The derogatory term "faggot," for example, now takes on the bitter tone of "old faggot."

There are additional problems faced by the older homosexual that are not encountered by most older people. Some have been refused insurance coverage. They may not be considered "immediate family" with the right of hospital visitations when their partner is ill. At death there may be no legal inheritance for the remaining partner and, even when a will is left, it can often be successfully contested by a family. There may be problems for the surviving "spouse" over property ownership as well as the inability of the survivor to sue in case of "wrongful death." If this were not enough, the remaining partner may be subjected to the prejudice, whether overt or subtle, of the loved one's family. The weight of this burden is borne at a time of great personal loss, as great as that experienced when any loved one dies.

Being homosexual in old age, in and of itself, is not what causes problems. Instead, it is society and the stigma attached to being homosexual that proves problematic. This is one reason that many homosexuals remain in the closet, and why unions among individuals who were not homosexual when young remain unrevealed. The preference is to present themselves publicly as roommates or friends. The climate for lesbians, at least, is changing toward less social censure. Whether this leads us to find that many older people have opted for a homosexual lifestyle (mostly due to loneliness) than is commonly realized, still remains to be seen. Only recently has it become necessary to differentiate between lesbians and gays with regard to social acceptance. Until AIDS burst upon the scene, the homosexual lifestyle was gaining greater acceptance or, at least, tolerance. Since AIDS can be transmitted through activity of homosexual males and not lesbians, social acceptance of gay men has suffered a setback.

Let us now add to our list of myths about sexuality, begun in chapter 1, some fictions about older homosexuals. These have been suggested by Bonnie Genevay in the edited work titled *Sexuality and Aging*:[1]

1. Older lesbians have more choice of partners because there are more older women than men.

It is easy to see how this myth perpetuates itself, given the increasing numbers of women compared to men in our society. But how does a lesbian know that another woman is interested in a relationship? Traditionally, it is the man who makes the moves. It is the man who can face the reality of failure, whereas the woman has been conditioned not to take risks. Therefore, the older lesbian waits for an invitation that never comes, because the other woman is waiting for an invitation that also never comes.

2. Homosexuals, like heterosexuals, suffer from ageism and the double standard of aging.

Just as older heterosexual men seek out younger women as partners, so, too, older homosexual men seek out youthful partners, only to find that, ultimately, those prospective younger partners also prefer youth. This occurs in a society that honors, and places a premium on, the youthful. Lesbians, unlike gay men, tend to honor older women and use them as role models.

3. Older gay people have learned to deal with the heterosexual world and no longer mind being in the minority.

Coping with minority status probably always means that one must develop a tolerance for being the butt of jokes. As people become older, I am not so sure that tolerance develops but perhaps there is greater awareness of why those in the majority feel the need to "put down" others. As we age, strength of character and self-assurance produce in those with high self-esteem, whether heterosexual or homosexual, a willingness to defend who they are.

Some other myths, not mentioned in chapter 1, with which older homosexuals have had to deal are: homosexuals are "born that way"; homosexuals are more likely to be disloyal to their country; any lesbian would prefer a man; and homosexuals are a menace to society (involved in more child abuse and sex-related crimes than heterosexuals). It is myths such as these that may have caused an older man, when asked how homosexuality affected his life, to say:

> This is like asking what it would be like . . . would your life have been any different if your eyesight was slightly defective, or if you had one lame leg. The answer is that it's in the background of everything you do. I

> feel that it (homosexuality) has created a narrower horizon than life would otherwise have had for me. I feel also that because of it, I have used in my life less initiative than I would otherwise have. I have been, in a sense, not crippled, but cramped because of it.[2]

Our culture tends to label. Whether manifested by calling someone a schizophrenic, a homosexual, or a hyperactive child, we seem to feel more comfortable with the ease and efficiency that labels provide. In the case of mental illness, historically this was not always so. The early records of older people residing in psychiatric facilities describe their behavior in minute detail. Today, however, once a label is stamped on a particular behavior, it is presumed to "tell all." That label has tremendous endurance; it stays with the individual for a lifetime, whereas a description of behavior may vary over time. In some societies there is no label for homosexuality, but only an observation, if even that, of a difference in sexual behavior. Consider the following report from an interview:

> One woman in her early sixties was intimately involved with another woman. This relationship, she said, has been one of the most tender and fulfilling relationships in her life. Neither she nor her partner consider themselves lesbians. Both have been married and still occasionally have male lovers. "We just prefer each other's company," she said, "and we thank each day that we found each other to love and share the remaining days of our lives."[3]

Stop for a minute and test yourself. What did you think as you read this? Did you say to yourself, "Who are they kidding? Of course, they're lesbians!" Or did you say, "In my way of thinking, there's no doubt in my mind that they are bisexuals!" Or are you one of the few who had no need to label at all? If we must label, then the bisexual statement does apply, but why label at all? When we attach labels to our sexuality it's as though we are defining a total person by that label; as though that makes everything about us different from others when, in fact, we are really only describing one facet that is different.

A friend of mine is, among many other descriptives, a counselor, a male, a son, a leader, an activist, a caregiver, a humorist, and a homosexual. The counselor part of him is evident as he talks with my human sexuality class each semester. He asks the students to form a circle, and, in this relaxed atmosphere, true sharing begins. One question he is usually asked is, "Why are you a homosexual?" His response is to ask the student why he or she is heterosexual. The point of his reply is that the only thing people really care about is his homosexuality, not why he is a counselor or any of the other attributes he possesses. Heterosexuality does not become a label and, therefore, heterosexuals are asked why they become teachers or lawyers, or why they live in the suburbs instead of the city, or any number of other tidbits of information we deem interesting to find out about each other.

This labeling stays with homosexuals through old age and, since it is looked at as a negative label by society, it adds to the other negatives of aging. In America it is more negative to be black than white, a woman than a man, old than young, poor than rich, fat than thin, short than tall, homosexual than heterosexual. How many of these negatives do *you*, the reader, possess? How are *you* affected? How do *you* react? Do *you* find yourself becoming less tolerant of this negative labeling as *you* grow older? Do *you* find yourself saying, "So what if I'm fat," "I'm proud to be black," or "I feel strong as a woman!" So, too, I would expect the older homosexual to no longer be tolerant of "put downs" and society's derisive reactions but, instead, say: "This is me, not all of me, but a part of me. If that isn't fine with you, who cares? It's fine with me!"

This self-acceptance in old age is necessary to achieve Erik Erikson's stage of integrity versus despair. Integrity means looking back on your life and feeling satisfied rather than falling into the despair of regretting what your life has been.

Weinberg and Williams, in a study conducted in 1974, concluded that no support could be found for the common view that older homosexuals are poorly adjusted. In fact, older respondents tended to have better self-concepts and were more stable. As with heterosexuals, the perspective that young people have of their elders causes negative judgments, whereas older persons feel just fine about themselves.[4] Kelly, in 1977, found that older homosexual men preferred contact with men their own age but were less likely to be in permanent relationships than were younger men. In the fifty to sixty-five age group 50 percent were satisfied with their sex lives, while in the over sixty-five age group 83 percent expressed satisfaction.[5]

Raymond Berger, in his book, *Gay and Gray,* published in 1982, reported on the results of an interview and questionnaire study.[6] He found that as gay people grow older they maintain their interest in partners of the same sex. Adapting to aging is very similar to that of heterosexual couples. The same issues are faced: chronic disease that limits interest or capacity for sex, the death of a loved one, the loss of support systems, and fears about the loss of sexual attractiveness. Some differences did exist between older homosexuals and heterosexuals regarding adjustments to these changes. Society's limited response in providing satisfactory help to older homosexuals as they make these adjustments is more pronounced than it is for older heterosexuals who are not receiving adequate assistance themselves. Even though homosexuals are taxpayers throughout their working lives, they do not receive the quantity and quality of publicly funded social services. Their invisibility even within the gay community is encouraged both by their own desire to disengage from active participation and a lack of hospitality afforded them by younger homosexuals who dominate the gay community.

Interestingly, Berger found that some differences are more positive for homosexuals than for heterosexuals. For instance, older homosexuals appear to be more financially secure than their heterosexual counterparts. Perhaps this results from the need to become independent earlier and from the knowledge that he or she cannot expect support from children or from relatives who may be reluctant to help. Since the crisis of independence comes earlier for homosexuals, self reliance in old age is not the tremendous shock that many heterosexuals confront. Senior Action in a Gay Environment (SAGE) is one of an increasing number of organizations formed to be a support system for older gay men and lesbians who, it is estimated, exist in greater number than those persons living in nursing homes.

One of the generalizations drawn from Brecher's data, and reported in *Love, Sex, and Aging,* is that more men than women over age fifty have engaged in homosexual activities at some time in their lives, yet more women than men have felt sexually attracted to their own gender. Of 512 unmarried women in his study, only three were paired up with other women, whereas 30 of the 413 unmarried men were in relationships with other men. The latter is more reflective of the incidence of homosexuality in our society than is the former, however, so the predictive value of this data is limited. The generalization is nevertheless an interesting one.

Brecher included a discussion of homosexual relationships in his entire sample and found that only 56 of the entire sample of 2,402 men and just nine from his sample of 1,844 women considered themselves homosexual. One obvious finding from this, since our population is estimated to be 10 percent homosexual, would be that older homosexuals are not interested in sending in written responses to questionnaires unless conducted for homosexuals only, as was Berger's. This may support my view that elder homosexuals are ready to indicate thumbs down to a society in which they are not accepted and they are willing to follow this up by not answering its "silly" questions. It could also be a protest against labeling.

Interestingly, though, hundreds of the respondents who did not consider themselves homosexuals were willing to provide data concerning their homosexual interest and experiences. From this data, Brecher felt he was able to suggest why more men act upon their homosexual attractions than do women. He felt that since men have been conditioned to initiate, they are willing to do so in same-sex relationships, whereas women, who have been conditioned to wait for an invitation, continue to wait even when sexually attracted.[7] This concurs with Genevay's first myth.

As far as older people's views of homosexuality are concerned there is less acceptance than in younger generations. The Victorian upbringing they experienced, which younger generations have not been exposed to, is an obvious reason for this disparity. Older people, who tend to be less liberal in their own sexual behavior, are also less liberal in judging others. As it is with issues other than sexuality, socioeconomic status does play a significant role in tempering the social views of older persons: men and women who are better educated and have higher levels of income are more accepting of sexual practices that deviate from their own preferences. Their attitude is simple: two consenting adults may do whatever they like in private.

Many states still consider homosexuality a crime. The recent arrest and conviction in Georgia of two gay men in their own home illustrates the lack of acceptance that churns beneath the social surface. Although the American Psychiatric Association removed homosexuality from its list of mental illnesses, many people still consider it to be a form of insanity. Problems with employment, social ostracism, and imprisonment make it easy to understand why many homosexuals remain "in the closet." Since it is less likely that someone would be recognized as homosexual based upon his or her appearance, it follows that most, if not all, heterosexuals know someone who is homosexual yet are unaware of the person's sexual preference. Obviously, your parents were not exclusively homosexual, unless you were adopted, but there are children who have been confronted with the homosexuality or bisexuality of their parents later in life. It is important for family members to recognize that this may be an option for an older parent. How would you feel if your parents made such a choice? What is your level of acceptance?

The Starr-Weiner report agrees that homosexuality has little appeal as a personal life style for the present population of older people; however, 64 percent of their respondents said it is all right for those who choose it. Future generations of the elderly will have experienced the gay rights movement, the removal of homosexuality from the list of pathologies, and may have even tried homosexual experiences during the 1960s and 1970s, which were times of sexual experimentation. It is predicted that most women, by the year 2010, will have had some homosexual experience. Kinsey, in the 1930s and 1940s, found that 37 percent of American males had had some homosexual contact to the point of orgasm, and in a later study he found that 20 percent of the women in his sample had had homosexual experiences. If women born around the turn of the century found homosexual experiences an option, it does not take a clairvoyant to predict that the Woodstock generation may embrace this option in their later years when heterosexual options dwindle.[8]

A generation ago Kinsey observed:

> The world is not divided into sheep and goats. . . . It is a fundamental of taxonomy that nature rarely deals with discrete categories. Only the human mind invents categories and tries to force facts into separated pigeonholes. The living world is a continuum in each and every one of its aspects. The sooner we learn this concerning human sexual behavior the sooner we shall reach a sound understanding of the realities of sex.[9]

NOTES

1. Bonnie Genevay, "Age Kills Us Softly When We Deny Our Sexual Identity," in *Sexuality and Aging*, edited by Robert L. Solnick (Los Angeles: The University of Southern California Press, 1978), 20-21.

2. Fred A. Minnegerode and Marcy R. Adelman, "Elderly Homosexual Women and Men: Report on a Pilot Study," *The Family Coordinator* (October 1978): 455.

3. Sharna L. Striar and Kay S. Hoffman, "Sexual Rights of the Single Elderly," *Journal of Social Work and Human Sexuality* 3 (Fall 1984): 81.

4. Benjamin B. Wolman (ed.), *Handbook of Human Sexuality* (Englewood Cliffs, N.J.: Prentice-Hall, Inc., 1980), 139.

5. J. J. Kelly, "The Aging Male Homosexual: Myth and Reality," *The Gerontologist* 17 (1977): 328-32.

6. Raymond M. Berger, *Gay and Gray: The Older Homosexual Man* (Urbana, Ill.: University of Illinois Press, 1982), 193-202.

7. Edward M. Brecher, *Love, Sex and Aging: A Consumers Union Report* (Mt. Vernon, N.Y.: Consumers Union, 1984), 212-27.

8. Bernard D. Starr and Marcella Bakur-Weiner, *The Starr-Weiner Report on Sex and Sexuality in the Mature Years* (New York: McGraw Hill, 1981), 246-47.

9. A. C. Kinsey, W. B. Pomeroy, and D. E. Martin, *Sexual Behavior in the Human Male* (Philadelphia: W. B. Saunders Co., 1948), 639.

8

Families

Accepting Each Other as Sexual Beings

"Filial love, the love of children for their parents and for each other, grows out of their intimate home associations and training, the recognition that they are one, blood of their blood, life of their life, being of their being."

Eugenics, 1915

Family members accepting their elders as sexual beings is something most people have really never thought about. As parents we worry about teenage sexuality, but as children we rarely, if ever, think about the sexuality of our parents. The first time I gave this thought conscious expression was while writing a research paper for a graduate course in human sexuality. By that time I was over forty myself and my husband and I had three teenage daughters. As I researched the topic of sexuality and aging, at a time in the 1970s when relatively little had been published on the topic, I ran across an interesting study. Conducted at Illinois State University, it examined the feelings of 646 students regarding their parents' sexuality. The results showed that 90 percent of the students felt their parents were happily married and still in love;

furthermore, they believed that their parents maintained this happy state without the help of sex, or at least not much of it. These results seemed both amusing and sad.

Surveying students in my own human sexuality courses points out that rarely is any thought given to their parents as sexual beings. I do see a trend indicating that students have accepted the fact that their parents might have sex but would prefer not to think about it. The inability to think of our parents or grandparents as sexual beings may stem from Freud's description of the oedipal child, who firmly believes his or her parents are sexless. This oedipal taboo returns in later life and is applied by the same person, now older, becoming a self-fulfilling and self-defeating prophecy.

An interesting comment was offered by one of my daughters who, when realizing I would be writing this book, told me of a conversation between her younger sister and their father. I had just been certified as a sex counselor, and the youngest daughter wondered just how I could possibly know enough about sex to be a sex counselor. Her father replied, "You'd be surprised how much your mother knows!" I rather imagine that, even though my daughters can intellectualize about their mother as a "sex expert," it is just as difficult for them to imagine their father and me having sex as it is for other children to imagine the same about their parents.

We may listen to some very poetic songs regarding growing old together, such as: "Through the years, through all the good and bad . . . I know what life's about by loving you through the years." This song is as popular with younger people as it is with their elders. The image produced may be of two aging people, who have loved each other for years, holding hands and smiling, perhaps gently kissing each other on the cheek. But could we imagine these same two elders lying in bed nude, having intercourse? No, no, no! Shocking. Repulsive. Not my mother and father! Certainly not my grandmother and grandfather!

Very slowly, though, some deterioration of this psychological blockade is occurring. Bumper stickers now proclaim, "I'm not a dirty old man, I'm a sexy senior citizen."

Communication in families can affect childhood perceptions of adult sexuality. In families where there is open communication children tend to feel that their parents have more sexual activity. Even for these children, though, it seems easier to imagine other older adults having sex rather than those in their own families. These offspring still report lower rates of presumed parental sexual intercourse or sexual intimacy of older adults than the actual rates of occurrence indicated by Kinsey's survey results or even more recent surveys.

The secret of parental sexuality has probably been one of the most successfully kept of all time. Children may find out the "secrets" of other family affairs, such as income level or that Uncle Jim is gay, but it takes longer for them to arrive at the remarkable discovery that their parents must have had sex, at least enough times to produce one offspring and maybe a sibling or two. But since that brings a shudder of disbelief, they would prefer not to think there were many more times than absolutely necessary. It usually is a little easier to think of Dad as having sex, since that is expected of men, but not good old Mom. That's almost unpatriotic and a blemish on the character of the very person who is synonymous with apple pie and all that is good in the world. Here, again, is the idea that sex is dirty and Mom must remain untainted by anything "evil."

Sex education classes are offered for the young but not for the middle-aged or the old. This leads one to believe that the only purpose of education is to provide information about birth control. It keeps sex tied to procreation and not the sexual expression of loving people who happen to be beyond the age of reproduction. As parents we are, or should be, concerned about all aspects of sex education for our children. Wouldn't it be a significant step forward if we became concerned about our parents' sex education and even our own? Can we imagine a time in the future when our children would sign *us* up for sex education classes? The fact that we have had children evidences little correlation with what we know about sex, given the large amount of misinformation we pass on to our children.

When asked to speak about matters pertaining to sexuality and aging, I generally find myself addressing those who work with elders but not the older persons themselves. Several years ago offered to teach a course on sexuality to a summer Elderhostel group. Elderhostelers are older adults who stay on college campuses for a week or two and take noncredit courses. My offer was not accepted by the younger administrators of the program; the reason given was that they did not think the Elderhostelers would be interested. Humbug! There is no doubt in my mind that they would be interested, but getting them to sign up for the course is another matter. I suspect that, if we could see into everyone's living room, a very large percentage of Dr. Ruth Westheimer's television audience would be composed of older people, sitting there and having a grand time hearing and thinking about sex. The difference is that, although they may be lonely, they were also more comfortable sitting there alone. They didn't have to sign up for a class, which would let everyone know they were interested in sex. Nor did they need to feel uncomfortable with others around them. Remember that this generation of elders was taught that it is improper to talk about personal matters outside the family and, since sex wasn't talked about *within* the family, how could they admit they wanted to know more about it?

On just one occasion have I been invited to speak to a group composed solely of elders. This was part of a senior citizens' day that offered several topics from which choices could be made to attend workshops at various scheduled times. My workshop on sexuality and aging, although well attended, did not have the number of participants who gravitated toward sessions that dealt with the usual topics of adjusting to retirement, making out your will, and similar areas of concern. Several of the participants told me later that many *wanted* to come forward but were afraid that the friends who accompanied them would think they were interested in sex. I could just picture a group of older people coming to the sign-up desk, looking around furtively to see if anyone is watching, and only signing up if they could do it without anyone noticing. I heard that a few who had entered my workshop late had in fact, ducked out of workshops they had originally signed up for and entered mine when their friends wouldn't know. I wonder if they ran back to the original workshop to meet their friends in the hallway. The "excitement" of this venture may have provided the pleasure of a clandestine affair—well, almost. Fortunately, though, there were many sexually open adults who combined with the more tentative group and we had a great time!

The newspaper covered this workshop as though it were a major event. This is another indication that sex is not considered a natural part of aging, but rather something sufficiently unique to be newsworthy.

My husband surprised me by sliding into the back row as I was introduced. I decided not to let him get by with anonymity and introduced him before I began. He stood up and stated that he came to see if I "practice what I preach." I wondered if maybe he was more interested in knowing if I preached what I practice! His comment set the tone for the whole workshop and was even quoted in the newspaper article. All in all, it was a wonderful workshop but, as I said, of the many, many presentations I have given over the years, this still remains the only one presented exclusively to elders.

There are many older people who could really educate their families about sex if relatives would only ask. One such elder says that her children know about her sexual liaisons and she finds their reactions to her life style "interesting, amusing, and touching. . . . Their major concern has been that I might get hurt, or be too generous with my material possessions." She said she had a minor family problem when her young grandson was visiting at the same time that her lover was there, and her grandson behaved like "a brat." He was jealous. Granny was supposed to be *his* for three weeks. I've read of this happening to young . . . mothers, but certainly never expected to encounter it at 66. My (lover) and I were most amused."

What if this "granny" wanted to remarry? What are the reactions of families to the remarriage of a parent or grandparent? Single or widowed parents who live with younger relatives are often made to feel guilty, if not indecent, for even wanting to date. Yet men and women are getting married—or remarried—in increasing numbers. Recent studies tell us that in a single year there are more than 16,000 brides and 33,000 grooms who are sixty-five years of age or older. Most couples who marry in their later years report that they had to overcome the objections and concerns of their children, their friends, or both.

Our culture often frowns upon late marriages. Perhaps those children who seek to prevent the marriage of an elderly widow or widower are afraid of losing an inheritance, or they may think it is unseemly. Elders who are themselves concerned about fairness with respect to financial matters, might deal with this by carefully preparing their wills so that assets prior to their marriage remain their own and anything that accrues after their marriage becomes joint property. This seems fair in light of the contributions that were made when a previous spouse was living.

As for the unseemly part of remarriage or of sexual intimacy, adult children can take major blame when they view their elders' normal urges for intimacy, romance, and commitment as evidence of a second childhood and therefore cause for social disgrace. Many children are much more comfortable suggesting that their parents or grandparents take up a hobby or become more involved in their families, that the elders provide household and baby sitting services, rather than encourage them to enter the mainstream of life through an intimate relationship. Some of this intolerance for parental sexuality may stem from hidden resentment caused by repressed childhood feelings regarding sexual needs that went unfulfilled: "If you didn't let me, why should I let you?" All of a sudden their parents seem to be acting in a sexually liberated way in which they as children had never been permitted to indulge.

As families are becoming more mobile, often with members living considerable distances from each other, this preoccupation with the sexuality of a family member is beginning to dissipate. The mobile elderly are able to free themselves from the "good will" of their offspring when it comes to sexual activity, much like what happens when a child leaves home. Within the home environment, parents have minute concerns about what the child is doing at any moment. Once the child has moved away or left for college, there is no way of knowing his or her every move and, therefore, there is a lessening of specific concern as to where the child is or what the child is doing at any given moment.

I surveyed my students, most of whom are around twenty years of age, concerning what they would like to know about their parents' sexuality. What follows is a sampling of some of their statements, which are presented in virtually unedited form:

> "I would like to know why my parents hid their sexuality so well. I really did believe, for awhile, they had sex five times (four kids and one miscarriage)."

> "Although children seem to have a hard time accepting their parents' sexuality, what I am interested in is how parents react when their child actually confronts them with this. For instance, parents often become uncomfortable when sexual situations come up in

front of their children. Some parents almost encourage their children to see them as asexual people."

I found this last sentence especially interesting. In other words, we encourage the asexual image.

"I never thought much about my parents having sex, because they hid the fact so well in front of me."

"I would like to find out how parents (especially mine) kept their intimate feelings inside without expressing them in any form in the presence of their children. I am 22 years old and still don't believe my parents are sexually active. They are in their 50s and in good health; I often wonder why their expression of intimacy is so hidden."

"When you think of your parents, you would think that they probably had sex four times because they only have four kids. That is the way most kids think, but I think it is cute if parents continue their sexual relationship."

I would like to bring attention to the word "cute," which is often used when describing what older people do. In effect, it relegates them to the period of childhood when so much that a child does is described as "cute." The sexual behavior of a young adult is not described as cute, but those same adults, now older, but doing the same things, have their behavior so described. I suppose cute is better than any number of derogatory adjectives that could be employed, but it does seem inappropriate for mature adults.

"I can relate to the title of your book (*My Parents Never Had Sex*) because I was never able to imagine my parents as sexual beings . . . . I believe that many parents and elderly people who are still sexually active feel that they must hide or be embarrassed by their sexuality, even to the extent of hiding it from their children."

"My own parents were never open about talking about sex and love within the family home. My mother always told me and my sister that 'the bed broke' when we were conceived, so basically we always thought sex was *dirty*. When we were teenagers my mother never wanted to discuss with us anything related to sex. I felt so naive when dating and in school. I would play along so as not to be outcast from my friends. I would like to find what others' experiences are. I hope they are different than mine, as I still feel somewhat naive with my sheltered life."

"When I think of my parents' sexuality, I perceive it as a sad situation. My dad is a very affectionate, 'huggy-kissy' kind of person, while my mom is a lot more reserved. One of my earliest memories is that of my mom saying, 'Not in front of the children.' (I never could figure out what Dad was doing that she didn't like.) I like to be hugged and kissed, so why didn't Mommy? I thought that she didn't like my father very much. And looking back on it, I may have been right."

One student wondered why a youngster or an adolescent would feel that his or her parents never had sex, and suggested the following reasons:

1. No display of affection between parents (in front of the children).
2. Parents never talked about such things with their children (i.e., not proper).
3. Parents did not sleep in or share the same bed (i.e., had separate beds in one room or slept in two different rooms).

Another student wondered what her parents did in their intimate moments together:

"Do they talk sweetly, stare into each other's eyes, whisper . . . or do they just do what there is to be done because it is part of married life and part of their regular routine? Do they have sex every third Tuesday of the month or is it spontaneous? In sum, is it the same as when they were younger, before the kids, etc.?"

The following student's comment indicates a change in perception:

> "I never think of my parents as sexual beings. I have a tough time imagining them as each other's 'lover.' I honestly used to believe they only had sex four times (once for each of us). Now I'm able to see their bond. I notice them making eye contact, that I suppose has special meaning for them. I still can't imagine them making love and I honestly don't feel I should concern myself with that. I do wonder if they enjoy sex like they used to when they were younger."

Some students made very positive statements about their parents' sex lives. This student added a qualifier, however.

> "I have a hard time *not* thinking my parents ever had sex because they are always so lovey-dovey except for when they're fighting, of course."

The following comments take a very nonageist approach:

> "I used to try not to think of my parents having sex, but now, as I've grown, I can accept it. I see them as exciting and vivacious individuals and appreciate the fact that they are still so much in love. But then again, there are some individuals that I can't picture together—and they don't necessarily have to be old. Some of my own friends in my age group pictured together can be pretty revolting! So, because of this, I don't think it's only age related. Perhaps in your book you can mention that it's not age that matters in all cases and that people have to learn to overcome these stereotypes." (Good suggestion!)

A nontraditional student, in her thirties, wrote:

> "I feel that having open communication about sexual matters with my parents and even now with my dad and his new wife, has provided me with a healthy and uninhibited view of sexuality. I wish that more parents were more open with their families about sexual matters."

Educating students about sexuality and aging has considerable effect. The following comments are illustrative of those made at the end of the course:

> "I think sex for older people is more a part of their life style than I ever thought it was."
>
> "I think sex for older people is a wonderful thing. It should be encouraged as being healthy and very good for two people no matter what their age is. Sex is an expression of two persons' feelings and should be allowed to continue as long as these two persons' are not being hurt by it."

Certain problems were identified by the younger respondents as stumbling blocks in the paths of older persons who seek to express their sexuality. One of the most frequently mentioned was the problem of families not being able to understand the older person's feelings. Others were the loss of a spouse, living in a nursing home, meeting people, feeling free of guilt for being intimate, illness, and lack of privacy if living with relatives. Some were concerned about too much sex having a negative effect on the health of older people (a topic that will be discussed in the next chapter). One student mentioned that older people are especially lonely and need sex just as much, if not more, than those who are younger. Another suggested that there is a stigma attached to older people who are sexually active. If they are active, they are thought to be "sex crazed" or promiscuous. This student pointed out how closely these feelings parallel those of parents about their teenagers' sexual activity. In general, the best solution to these problems is to allow older people to do what they please (sexually). If it isn't hurting anyone else, there's nothing wrong with it.

When 40 students were asked to complete this sentence, "When I think of my parents having sex, I feel . . .," the following results were obtained: 21 positive (great, happy, okay, glad, etc.); 7 negative, (confused, embarrassed, etc.); 5 no answer; 7 ambivalent (happy but embarrassed). Apparently it is more difficult for these same students to think of their grandparents as having sex. When "grandparents" was substituted for "parents," the results were: 15 positive, 9 negative; 15 no answer; and 1 ambivalent. Many of the 15 no answers indicated that they had no grandparents living as couples. This brings us right back to the problem of the single person (usually Grandma) in old age.

Families who want to understand and even encourage the sexuality of any older members might find it helpful to identify the breakdown of sexual expression in the elderly by examining the Geriatric Sexuality Breakdown Syndrome (SBS) as proposed by Merrie Jean Kaas. The steps in this syndrome are as follows:[2]

1. Precondition of susceptability—identity problem; diminished ego strength; physiological changes in response cycle.
2. Dependence on current cues—cues from sexual taboos and myths of geriatric sexlessness; few aged role models; sex is primarily for procreation; Oedipal conflict (observing or imagining parents engaging in sex creates high levels of anxiety); fear of young that their abilities will be lost with age leads to discounting importance of sex in later years.
3. Societal labeling—dirty old men; indecent old woman.
4. Sick role—role of perverse old person; sick; abnormal sexual drives.
5. Learning or behavior skills—verbally disavow any sexual desires or activity, thus decreasing sexual activity.
6. Atrophy of social skills—loss of sexual performance skills for sexual excitement and enjoyment.
7. Self labeling—self perception as dirty old man or woman; identification as asexual.

The family can intervene in this cycle by helping to change society's cues or by helping elders cope with the negative cues. Much of this can be accomplished through education. Elders can be helped to understand physiological changes, the influence of medication they may be taking, and specific touching techniques.

Accurate information must also be given to healthcare professionals and family members. One such intervention that I conducted was a series of workshops for professionals who work with the elderly.[3] These were offered at the Center for the Study of Aging at the University of Buffalo. I was able to report a statistically significant change in knowledge about sexuality and aging, along with a trend that indicated a change in attitudes. It is hoped that this book, if read by the whole family, (for whom it is intended) will also encourage a greater understanding of an older family member's sexuality so that the cycle of misinformation and misperception can be broken.

The expression of love is a human need shared by all family members; it should not be based upon the number of years one has lived. Family members need to realize that each individual is a sexual being from birth until death. Obviously that does not mean having intercourse at birth, or in early childhood. "Sexual being," therefore, means something far more encompassing than intercourse. In our Western society we might describe this in terms of love. That is a major part of our sexuality—expressing love and being able to love someone else. Reaching out to someone, touching, and caring, all of these add to our sense of self. No matter how old, each family member deserves the dignity that being fully human requires of all who live in civilized society.

NOTES

1. Edward M. Brecher, *Love, Sex, and Aging: A Consumers Union Report* (Mt. Vernon, New York: Consumers Union 1984), 193.

2. Merrie J. Kass, "Geriatric Sexuality Breakdown Syndrome," *International Journal of Aging and Human Development*, 13 (1981): 71-77.

3. Doris B. Hammond and Warren C. Bonney, "Results of Sex Education for Support Persons Working with the Elderly," *Journal of Sex Education and Therapy* 11 (1985): 42-45.

9

Health and Sexuality

Does It Help or Hurt?

"A foolish notion sometimes prevails that it is necessary to health to have frequent intercourse. There is no condition of life more thoroughly in accordance with perfect vigor than chaste celibacy. Next to this comes moderation in married life. It is never required for sanitary reasons to abuse the privileges which law and usage grant. Any such abuse is pretty sure to bring about debility and disease."

Eugenics, 1915

Humankind's search for the fountain of youth and its desire to live to a ripe old age have provided a mixed bag of positive and negative results. As we dramatically increase the years of life expectancy through better medical care and nutrition, we increase the possibility of illness during those additional years. The longer we live, the more chance there is for disability.

Unfortunately, if society deems the old to be asexual, think how this is compounded by being *disabled.* The facts of human physiology and statistical probability over time increase the chances for this combination to occur. The older we are the less resistance we have to illness, the longer it takes to recuperate, and the greater the incidence of chronic disease. Since good health is significantly related to feelings of pleasure and satisfaction, our state of mind can have an enormous impact on the state of our health.

Many people believe that illness marks the beginning of the end of sexual activity. To a degree this is true: the trauma of disease causes the body to summon up energy to fight off illness and thus little energy is left for sexual outlets. A chronic illness can produce the same effect but for a much longer period of time.

Recovery from acute illness may be sufficiently rapid, therefore not altering the patient's sense of sexual self and his or her level of sexual activity can be resumed with little or no interruption. Chronic illness may produce greater levels of anxiety as the patient learns to "live with" and adjust to the permanence of a disability. Illness, accident, or surgery may cause an alteration in a patient's concept of his or her body image. This may require a sympathetic physician who is willing to deal with sexual matters, a supportive family, and especially a supportive sexual partner. Counseling may also be needed; in fact it should probably be considered an indispensable part of the recovery process.

Even though impaired health may affect sexual functioning, it must be remembered that old age by itself causes a slowed response. Some studies have indicated that declines in sexual activity are related more to aging than they are to health. The two factors together produce the greatest effect.

It is important for each of us to have at least a general knowledge of the various disabilities that are more likely to occur in the older population and how these conditions may or may not affect sexual interest and ability. This information is vital for everyone, old, young, and all ages in between. Each of us is growing older and will someday need to put this knowledge to good use. Most of us also face the possibility of providing primary or secondary care to an ill person, either as a family member or as a service provider.

It is also important for us to realize the natural developmental changes of aging so that these are not confused with disease states. We truly begin to live in a baggy suit as connective tissues lose their elasticity and the relentless force of gravity continues its downward pull.

Eyelids, ear lobes, chin, breasts, upper arms, buttocks, and thighs begin to sag as they gradually soften. To illustrate, compare the present shape of your face to your high school graduation picture. It has begun to elongate and wrinkles have set in. One good natured friend of mine joked that she went to a fortune teller who offered to read her face. Greying of the hair occurs, despite President Reagan's protests to the contrary, and pigmentation patches, commonly called "age spots," occur. These "conditions" are caused by natural aging processes but are treated almost as diseases by those who react most strongly to our youth-worshipping culture. Just listen carefully to cosmetics advertisements for fade creams and the like.

It may be that some will opt for cosmetic surgery by having a facelift, mammoplasty (breast implant), or even a total body lift. Hairpieces, hair transplants, and hair dying are popular means of responding to the call of youth. The biggest disappointment is when the hoped for miracles do not occur. It's like the advertisement that implicitly promises to make wonderful things happen by owning a particular make of automobile. People buy the car and sit around waiting for things to happen—and they're still sitting there, waiting. It may be depressing to have sagging skin, but at least you have an excuse while you are waiting. How *really* depressing it must be to find out that your nice tight skin did nothing to improve your bitchy personality, which is what your problem was in the first place.

Aging itself is a disease state only if you allow it to be. However, since there is a greater chance of actual health problems in old age, let's look at the more likely conditions. Butler and Lewis,[1] Hogan,[2] and Hobson[3] provide a comprehensive overview of possible medical problems and their sexual ramifications.

Heart Disease

Although heart disease is more prevalent among men than women, after menopause the rates begin to reach parity. There is an unsubstantiated fear that one will have a heart attack while making love. Actually, fewer than one percent of heart attacks occur during sexual activity and about 70 percent of that 1 percent occurred when having sex with a partner other than your own. Newspaper accounts of such occurrences have led us to believe that there is a far greater percentage of these induced coronaries. Such extremely rare occurrences become newsworthy when they involve a person of prominence. This is much like our incorrect belief that crimes, including rape, occur more often among the elderly when actually the reverse is true. It is just that it makes for more horrifying news, and subsequent reader interest, when it is a little old lady being victimized.

Depression may set in after a heart attack, thereby placing sexual activity on a back burner. Physically, however, most physicians say that sexual activity may be resumed as soon as the patient is able to walk up two flights of stairs. Until then, touching and caressing can be a very important part of love-making during the intervening months of recuperation.

Physicians need to discuss sexuality directly with a heart patient and with his or her partner. Unfortunately, some physicians do not, cannot, or will not do this. Medical schools are beginning to provide for and require training in human sexuality; however, some physicians did not receive it as part of their medical education and may be reluctant to bring up what they consider a sensitive issue. That means it may be necessary for the patient to ask questions. The subject, therefore, may never come up, either because the patient and/or physician feel uncomfortable broaching the subject or due to the automatic assumption that heart attacks do, in fact, mean a permanent halt to sexual activity.

Sexual activity can actually provide some mild exercise and help to relieve tension, both of which are healthy for the heart attack patient. People seem to think that sexual intercourse requires superabundant amounts of energy when all one really needs is the same amount of energy necessary for many other daily activities.

High Blood Pressure and Stroke

High blood pressure requires medication and monitoring by a physician if a stroke is to be avoided. What is often not realized is that the medication prescribed for high blood pressure results in secondary impotence in a few people and mild sexual response difficulties in many others. A sudden rise in blood pressure can cause a stroke if one's current blood pressure level is already above normal. It's unlikely that sexual activity can cause a stroke, but it is always better to talk this over with a physician.

If paralysis results from a stroke, it is important that instructions be given for alternate sexual positions as well as counseling related to problems of adjusting to an altered body image.

Cancer

A diagnosis of cancer is so shocking that the individual's sexuality, although not affected by the cancer as such, is affected by the depression and anxiety that the diagnosis precipitates. It is at this time, more than ever, that the individual needs the touching and caring that sexual expression brings. Often, however, the partner will feel that he or she is being insensitive to the condition or, in some cases, individuals even think that cancer is catching. On a recent television program a woman, married seventeen years, told how she was not only faced with the diagnosis of cancer but with a husband who was so afraid of the disease that he would not touch her. Even though her prognosis was positive for remission, she not only had to adjust to her condition but had to make plans for ending a marriage.

Diabetes

Diabetes has in the last forty years become so well managed that young people, who at one time rarely survived to their mid-twenties, are now active adults and parents. The onset of diabetes late in life is of concern because its incidence is on the rise, but contracting the disease does not automatically lead to male impotence as has been thought. Sex therapy has helped to reverse impotence in diabetic men. However, when all management techniques fail, chronic impotence may occur. Since sexual interest and desire is usually retained, it is important that alternatives to intercourse be suggested.

Considerably less has been reported about the sexual effects of diabetes in women since their sexual ability is not dependent upon achieving an erection. There is little impaired orgasmic response, and diabetic women have the same reduced lubrication and diminished elasticity of the vaginal wall that is experienced by women not so afflicted. Therefore, vaginal cream, jelly, or saliva may help.

Arthritis

There are two types of arthritis: osteoarthritis and the rheumatoid form, with the former being the milder of the two. Osteoarthritis is usually noninflammatory and rarely interferes with sexual activity. Only when the disfigurement results in emotional reactions of anger or embarrassment does this lead to what would be called a psychologically induced sexual problem.

The second type, known as rheumatoid arthritis, is much more severe. It can cause excruciating pain. If medication does not relieve the pain enough to provide for sexual intercourse, and if joint and muscle exercises, rest, and warm baths do not provide sufficient relief, it is advisable for both partners to receive counseling. This should include advise for alternate positions that could make sexual intercourse more comfortable. It has been shown that sexual intercourse actually can help to ease the pain of arthritis, probably by the adrenal gland's production of cortisone. For continued relief, however, this sexual activity must occur every four hours, much like a scheduled dose of medication. Since that is rather unlikely to happen, one will have to be satisfied with only occasional relief through this particular "prescription." Additionally, since sexual dissatisfaction can lead to stress, which aggravates arthritis, a vicious cycle occurs. Mainly it is important for an arthritic to lead as active and fulfilling a life as is possible.

Backache

As in the case of arthritis, sexual activity can be of benefit to the backache sufferer. Backaches are suffered more by older adults. This may be from improper lifting, overexertion, slipped discs, arthritis, osteoporosis, or other causes. A firm mattress will help, as will exercise. Many older people are finding, as have sports enthusiasts of all ages, that chiropractic is an excellent help for backaches when self help methods fail. Chiropractic has also become a respected preventive measure. Today's educated chiropractors have received many years of preparation and practice in order to be certified. My eighty-two-year-old mother received immediate relief at the hands of a chiropractor for a back problem, and it has not recurred. She tells me that many of her friends have similar success stories to tell.

During sexual activity, a pillow placed under the area of discomfort may help. Using the side position during intercourse or having the backache sufferer assume the bottom position may also be helpful. Sexual activity is an excellent exercise for the back, stomach, and pelvic muscles.

Anemia

Loss of appetite and headaches can drain energy and cause loss of interest in sex. Anemia is frequent to some degree in many older adults, about 25 percent of whom are affected. This is one of the reasons for having regularly scheduled comprehensive medical examinations.

Hernia or Rupture

A hernia or rupture results form the protrusion of a part of the intestine through the abdominal wall. This causes a cutting off of the blood supply, a type of strangulation that results in tissue death. Straining increases the pain. Although sexual intercourse does not often induce strangulation, there is strain involved. Surgery may be recommended to avoid an emergency. Normal sexual activity can be resumed after healing has taken place.

Parkinson's Disease

Tremors, slowness, some facial paralysis, and changes in posture and gait are indicators of Parkinson's Disease, a progressive nerve disorder that usually occurs during the later years and is often accompanied by depression. It is the depression that can lead to lack of sexual interest in both men and women and to impotence in men. In the later stages of the disease the impotence may become physiologically induced.

Chronic Prostatitis

This condition (inflammation of the prostate gland) affects men and is sometimes accompanied by a feeling of embarrassment, since it is alternately blamed on too little or too much sex. The condition does cause diminished sexual interest because there is pain in the perineal region (between the scrotum and the anus) and in the penis when urination and ejaculation occur. The prostate gland, located below the bladder, secretes the fluid that transports sperm during sexual intercourse. Sexual interest usually returns after treatment, which consists of antibiotics, warm sitz baths, and periodic gentle massage by a physician.

Stress Incontinence

A urine seepage, caused by a falling of the bladder, may occur when women cough, sneeze, laugh, engage in sexual intercourse or in some other form of exertion. This is more likely to occur in women who have had a number of children, often with unrepaired injuries during childbirth, or who have had a hysterectomy. It becomes more of a problem as women grow older, often necessitating the wearing of a sanitary napkin at all times. The problem is so common that special pads are now on the market designed to be used for this type of incontinence. A physician may suggest the hormone estrogen, taken orally or applied locally as a cream. In extreme cases surgery may be indicated. Kegel exercises, as described earlier, are almost always recommended. These exercises should begin when a woman is young, as a preventive measure.

Peyronies' Disease

This is a relatively uncommon disease in men and involves the incorrect angling of the penis: it has an upward bowing with the shaft angled off to the right or the left. The cause is unknown but the symptoms result from a fibrous thickening of the walls of the blood vessels of the penis. Symptoms usually disappear spontaneously within four years. In most cases intercourse continues during this period but may result in a degree of discomfort; in extreme cases an inability to have intercourse may occur.

Alcoholism and Drug Use

Alcohol may help to lessen sexual inhibitions but at the expense of interfering with sexual performance. In other words, you want to but you can't. If your father or mother is already alcoholic, old age may aggravate this condition through unoccupied time, loneliness, and depression. If your parent is not alcoholic, there is a possibility he or she may become one for these same reasons. When a person is not feeling gratified by life, alcohol can become a form of self-gratification. In men, alcoholism may cause partial erections, retarded ejaculation, or impotence. A woman may drink to cover up her unmet sexual needs, which she may be unwilling to confront and/or about which she may be unable to confide in anyone else. The history of alcoholism must be part of any evaluation of sexual dysfunction in an older couple, just as in a couple of any age.[4]

Many drugs and some diuretics have among their side affects impotence and sexual dysfunction. Even minor tranquilizers may cause enough muscle relaxation to make orgasms impossible for either or both sexes. Hypnotics (sleep inducers) not only cause sexual dysfunction but insomnia as well.

In the paragraphs that follow, we will consider certain surgical procedures in relation to their impact upon sexual performance.

Prostatectomy (Removal of Prostate Gland)

Over half of middle-aged and older men experience the previously described prostate problems, and half of these will need to have an operation. A common belief is that prostate surgery ends potency. That need not be the case, although it may alter ejaculatory sensation. The men affected are fully capable of sexual activity through retrograde (reversed) ejaculation where the semen is ejaculated as usual but enters the bladder and is then voided. Recovery from surgery takes a couple of months, after which men are able to fully resume sexual activity. *Should* impotence occur it is usually temporary. However, in some cases it may be organic and counseling will be needed to deal with this loss.

There are three types of prostatectomies, the most radical being the perineal, which is indicated when cancer is present or when the patient has an extremely enlarged prostate gland and, due to advanced age or complicating factors, is unable to withstand prolonged anesthesia. This is the type that is most likely to affect potency. If cancer is present, the testicles may have to be removed as well (orchiectomy). The loss of sexual organs that are directly related to masculinity may alter a man's sexual life style; counseling to regain self-image may be strongly indicated. The other two types of prostatectomies, transurethral resection (partial prostate removal through the penis) and the suprapubic procedures (in which surgery is performed just above the pubic bone area), rarely affect potency and, in fact, some men actually experience an increase in potency.

Hysterectomy

The term "hysterectomy" derives from the Greek word for hysteria (*hysterikos*), which means "suffering in the uterus." Therefore, to remove the uterus (womb) was to relieve the patient of hysteria. A word of caution is needed regarding this surgical procedure. In light of past bouts of unnecessary tonsillectomies and appendectomies being performed, many women are being cautioned about many unnecessary hysterectomies being scheduled. In fact, the United States has the highest hysterectomy rate in the world: two-and-one-half times that of England, and four times that of Sweden and some other European countries. Could it be that these countries' state-paid health plans have removed the economic incentive to perform unneeded surgery?[5]

With this cautionary note, let us discuss the therapeutic hystrectomies that occur and their effect on sexuality. There is no medical evidence that a hysterectomy causes a change in sexual desire or performance. However, the removal of a woman's ultimate symbol of femininity can bring to her mind thoughts of premature aging and loss of attractiveness. Older women may have considered removal of the uterus as female "castration": after the procedure they were rendered asexual and unable to have sexual intercourse. The uterus makes pregnancy possible but it has no effect on sexual intercourse. It is true, however, that the uterus does undergo a series of rhythmic contractions during orgasm.

If the ovaries are removed (ovariectomy), loss of the female hormone, estrogen, occurs and the woman, if she is not already postmenopausal, becomes menopausal. Since the first ovariectomy in 1809, "ovaries were routinely removed as a highly touted remedy for hysteria, psychological disorders, insanity, and even to keep women under the social control of men. These justifications for the performance of ovariectomies were used as recently as 1946."[6] This should be a challenge to women to take charge of their own health care and to realize that it has been based upon a male medical model. I challenge older women, especially, to remove physicians from pedestals, recognize them as the valuable healthcare technicians that they are, and speak with them about procedures related to good health. Older women need to feel respect for physicians but they also need to shed the conditioned awe and reverence with which they learned to treat the medical profession. Only in this way can an older woman develop a cooperative partnership with a physician regarding her own health.

The only absolute reason for a hysterectomy or ovariectomy is cancer. Benign fibroid tumors should not necessitate a hysterectomy, only if there is uncomfortable pain and bleeding. Many of these symptoms disappear at the onset of menopause. Only about 20 percent of hysterectomies are actually performed because of an indication of cancer.[7] When a woman does have a hysterectomy, and especially if it is cancer related, sensitive counseling is needed to adjust not only to the operation but to help with coping skills regarding the diagnosis of cancer itself.

Mastectomy

Because the breasts are an outward symbol of femininity, the adjustment to this loss may be more difficult than in the case of hysterectomy. Mastectomy is another operation that is expected to be performed less frequently as more physicians recommend that the cancer be removed in a more localized manner. This is why early detection is so vital.

It should be obvious that a mastectomy would constitute no physiological cause for sexual problems, but there sometimes are severe psychological problems. This severity is recognized by the formation of support groups, usually led by women who have had mastectomies themselves. A male colleague of mine has formed such groups for males as well, since men can have a crucial effect upon their wives'/partners' adjustment.

Ostomy

Colostomies (pertaining to the large bowel) and ileostomies (pertaining to the small bowel) are sometimes performed for cancer and other diseases of the intestinal tract. Part of the bowel (large intestine) is removed and the anus is closed. An artificial opening is made in the abdominal wall and a bag is attached. This bag fills with feces and must be emptied.

Ostomies should not physiologically interfere with sexual functioning, but there are obvious psychological adjustments to be made. There are sometimes embarrassing bowel sounds and odors but, for the most part, these can be controlled. Support groups can be of considerable help in allowing the individual and his or her partner to work through their feelings, their perceptions, and how they may need to revise their sexual relationship.

Coronary Bypass Surgery

Sexual adjustment after coronary bypass surgery is somewhat different for women than for men. Women tend to have less of a reduction in frequency of intercourse, though their sexual desire is more affected; in men it is their arousal. Women seem to have less performance anxiety and harbor fewer fears (e.g., that they will die during intercourse). In general, women seem to be better able, psychologically, to handle the surgery than are men.[8]

Excessively Enlarged Vagina

A type of plastic surgery may be needed when a woman has an excessively large vagina, a condition making intercourse, or a least its enjoyment, difficult. This may have been the result of bearing numerous children or from a difficulty arising in childbirth where tears occur in the opening of the vagina. Although more likely to manifest itself in older women, younger females may be affected as well. Surgery may be recommended if sexual enjoyment is problematic (a mental health concern) but would not be suggested for reasons of physical health.

Paraplegics and Quadraplegics

A book titled *Sexual Options for Paraplegics and Quadraplegics*[9] suggests that psychological orgasms (orgasms that yield pleasurable release without input from a penis or a vagina) are possible as well as direct sexual stimulation. One such method, which uses mental abilities to enhance sexual pleasure, is "alternate sensation," or "transfer of sensation." This method involves transposing sensations mentally by using the imagination to create a fantasy. The fantasy would be that physical sensation is occurring in an insensate area such as the genitals. Another mental effort proposed is "psychological orgasm" by which a disabled person can use memories from before the injury to achieve a pleasurable release of sexual tension, one that is different from physical, genital orgasm, but is satisfying and not necessarily inferior. Fantasies and physical sensations made possible by a partner or through masturbation could also be used to achieve this release. The authors claim that the climax experienced during these orgasms is not wholly mental and that there is some kind of change in the physical state. It is suggested that these techniques can bring pleasure to a wide range of sick and disabled people, not only para- and quadraplegics.

Handicapping conditions resulting from disease, surgery, or accident can affect both the ability and the desire for sexual activity. These disabilities, whether temporary or permanent, bring with them problems associated with change in body image, self-worth, and self-concept. Performance anxiety may also occur. There may be changes in function directly related to paralysis, incoordination, or spasticity. Incontinence and changes in sensation may also result.

Learning to cope with handicapping and/or debilitating conditions requires a critical examination of values and attitudes concerning sex. There may be "mechanical" problems in having sex, which are the result of deformity or weakness and pain. A variety of positions need to be tried to find the ones best suited for the specific situation or set of circumstances. In extreme cases helpers may need to be willing to place persons in positions for sexual intercourse. In some situations, caressing and oral stimulation may be encouraged.

Too often the assumption is made by the family of a physically challenged person that the sex drive is nonexistent ("challenged" is now the preferred descriptive word, rather than "disabled"). These loved ones forget that the same sexual drives exist now, even with the handicapping condition, as they did before any physical change took place. Feelings of hunger and thirst were not eliminated by the physically disabling condition. Likewise, there is no reason to assume that sexual feelings have diminished (unless there is physical or psychological evidence to support this assumption). The sexual needs must be evaluated in light of the manner and frequency with which they were expressed prior to the disability. A frank and personal approach needs to be taken.

There is a need to anticipate problems before an individual leaves the hospital. Sexual adjustment is definitely possible for physically challenged persons. This requires awareness, understanding, and aggressiveness on the part of health professionals, families, and the physically challenged person him or herself.

Although it has been several years now, I still remember vividly a woman who came to Marshall University in West Virginia to speak about sexuality and the handicpped. She was a paraplegic herself and in a wheelchair. Her body was crippled but her face, in contrast, was the most sensual I had ever seen. As she spoke frankly about how she communicated her sexual needs to her male partners, which included suggestions for their help in sexual positioning, I began to see not only the sensuality in her face but that of her entire person, making her crippled body virtually insignificant. If we allow ourselves to see a total sexual being rather than a person with defective parts, we encourage that person to see him or herself as a total sexual human being. This woman, whose name I have forgotten, permitted that to happen for me and I will always be grateful to her for it. Sexuality is not an action but an essence. The more we see the sexuality of others, the more that sexuality develops in ourselves. Likewise, the more we are able to see beyond age, handicap, or gender, the more obviously expressive our own sexuality becomes.

The adjustment of the disabled elderly is very much like the adjustment of the physically challenged in general. However, one is struck by the enormity of what our society would consider a compound handicap: being physically or mentally handicapped *and* being elderly.

We have spoken of physical handicaps, but what about those who are experiencing mental disturbances? Persons who have organic brain syndrome, such as Alzheimer's Disease often become institutionalized. (The topic of sexuality in institutions will be discussed in the next chapter.) Prior to institutionalization, families may notice sexual behavior that is inappropriate with regard to time, place, and social context. These behavior manifestations of dementia can be very upsetting. The person affected by this dread disease desperately needs touching, love, and affection, but it must be given in such a way that the confused person is somehow helped to see the limits of his or her sexual actions. This is difficult to get across and places enormous strain on family relationships. Limit-setting works best when the individual feels loved and cared for. Family members should be encouraged to hold the hand of the affected person, give plenty of hugs, or just simply touch the person, perhaps by reaching out and squeezing his or her shoulder while walking by. This type of touch should be accepted and encouraged from the affected person as well. Just as we have found that premature babies were lacking the sense of touch while in incubators and are now being provided with touching stimuli as normal procedure in the hospital, so, too, must we provide those of any age and condition with the therapeutic effects that being touched provide.

Lesser mental disturbances can also have strong effects on expressions of sexuality. Anxiety or depression can result from the loss of youthful attractiveness. Some people go through stages of grief at losing their youth, almost as though they have lost a person (themselves), a person they loved much more than this sagging, wrinkled individual whom they barely recognize when they look in the mirror. It is typical that, when we think of ourselves, the picture we see is that of someone around thirty-five years of age. This is perfectly normal. However, the person who cannot accept him- or herself as the same person reflected in the mirror has lost the self-love that is so necessary to feel loved by someone else: "If I don't feel lovable, then no one else must think I'm lovable." Anxiety and depression can result.

Depression is a common psychiatric disorder of the elderly. Mr. B was suffering from all the usual symptoms of depression, one of which is loss of sexual desire. Unless a counselor or family member is able to ask about the loss of sex interest just like he or she might ask about loss of appetite, this may go unnoticed. Mr. B's spouse, in the meantime, is experiencing terrible feelings of rejection.

Depressive reactions occur frequently in aged persons. It may follow the death of a loved one or the decline of self-esteem when a job or role is lost. Depression may be caused *by* physical illness or it may be the cause *of* physical illness, but it should be viewed as neither normal nor inconsequential in older persons. It is, however, the most common psychiatric disorder of old age, and usually its cloud does not lift spontaneously as is often the case with younger persons; the longer the depressive state lasts the more embedded and resistant it becomes. It can, in fact, be life threatening. The risk of suicide is greater, as is the overall mortality rate, among depressed persons. Sex difficulties occur as the depressed person no longer shows interest in sex and derives decreasing pleasure from sexual activities that were previously enjoyed.[10]

This chapter posed the question of whether sexuality can help or hurt the person in ill health. Sexuality, including sexual intercourse, has been found to have a positive effect on the health, both physical and mental, of older persons. Some studies indicate that it even increases life expectancy. Exercise in general, has been known to do that, and sex is certainly a form of exercise isn't it? Some disagree that there is an increase in life expectancy, but all agree that the quality of life is improved when we express our sexuality in some way. In other words, we will all die at some time, so it should be our goal as individuals to experience all there is of the good things in life, for as long as we can. When we are in ill health, probably more than at any other time, we need the warmth, caring, and touching that affirms us as human beings.

NOTES

1. Robert N. Butler and Myrna I. Lewis, *Sex After Sixty: A Guide for Men and Women for Their Later Years* (New York: Harper and Row, 1976), 26-51.

2. R. Hogan, *Human Sexuality: A Nursing Perspective* (New York: Appleton-Century-Crofts, 1980), 522-676.

3. Karen Hobson, "The Effects of Aging on Sexuality," *Health and Social Work* 9 (Winter 1984): 25-35.

4. Domeena C. Renshaw, "Geriatric Sex Problems," *Journal of Geriatric Psychiatry* 17 (1984): 123-38.

5. Robert S. Mendelsohn, *Male Practice* (Chicago: Contemporary Books, 1982), 99.

6. Ibid., 30.

7. Ibid., 99.

8. Stanley Athof, Candace Coffman, and Stephen Levine, "The Effects of Coronary Bypass Surgery on Female Sexual, Psychological, and Vocational Adaptation," *Journal of Sex and Marital Theory* 10 (Fall 1984): 176-84.

9. Thomas O. Mooney, Theodore M. Cole, and Richard A. Children, *Sexual Options for Paraplegics and Quadraplegics* (Boston: Little Brown and Co., 1965), 1-6.

10. Marguerite D. Kermis, *Mental Health in Later Life: The Adaptive Practice* (Boston: Jones & Bartlett Publishers, Inc., 1986), 9, 39, 188, 198.

10

Institutionalization

Sex Not Allowed Here!

"And we all think the very best place for you to go is to an old ladies' home somewhere, a real nice one, of course, where you could have your room and every comfort. You see you are too old to be running about the country, and too old to be of any use now to anybody anywhere. Don't you think that is the best thing you can do yourself?"

Eugenics, 1915

A newspaper account told of the dying wish of an eighty-two-year-old man who asked that his family understand why he shot and killed himself and his crippled wife. The administrator of the nursing home where they were found said that they just didn't want to live without each other. It was a Romeo and Juliet story, only the main characters were old rather than in the blush of youth. Mrs. I, at eighty, had been living in a nursing home suffering a disabling stroke. She could not walk and had arthritis. Her husband, who recently learned he had cancer, visited her daily so they could share meals. They loved each other, were always holding hands, and were always together. A note left by Mr. I, and discovered by police on a desk in the couple's apartment located near the nursing home, implored relatives to consider his action "not as an act of violence, but an act of love."

Obviously these two older people wanted to feel in control of their lives to the very end. Nursing home placement often signifies the end of control. Let's imagine that both Mr. and Mrs. I had ended up in a nursing home together. Would members of their family have checked to see what arrangements could be made so that they might continue a loving and sexual relationship if they so desired? I doubt it. Many concerned family members conscientiously use check lists to help them determine the quality of a nursing home they are considering. I have seen some very fine check lists prepared for that purpose, but rarely have I seen one that indicates anything about sexual privacy. I advise you to add that to your list. It may be far more important to your older relative than you imagine.

The residents in nursing homes, when considering their sexual needs, are truly a forgotten and neglected population. These people may lead lives of quiet desperation. Unlike the general population in which most sexual activity is behind closed doors, those who reside in nursing homes are living in glass houses. Probably more often than we realize, sexual activity is taking place, but think of the clandestine maneuvering this involves and the subsequent feelings of guilt.

Nursing homes can deprive residents of their sexual rights, and frequently they lead celibate lives. Residents are separated by gender and only permitted to mingle in the dining hall or lounge. I wonder what future generations, who were used to co-ed dormitories, will say about this when some of *them* enter nursing homes. I suspect the problem will take care of itself by that time, but why should residents have to wait for such liberation? At least the separation of married couples is becoming less frequent, unless they request to be separated (as some have done). But even when married couples occupy the same room, are they provided with a double bed as they have been used to? Of course not! The usual single beds suffice for everyone. Not only is nighttime the best, and perhaps only, time for couples to snuggle together, but if they both have to get into a single bed in order to do it, it's a real safety hazard! I wonder how many broken bones have happened in that way.

Although only five percent of our population reside in nursing homes or skilled care facilities at any one time, over ten percent can expect to be in such a home at some point in their lives. Since the over eighty-five age group is the fastest growing sector in our population, we can expect these figures to rise. We are not, therefore, talking about an insignificant number of people who may be affected by nursing home regulations.

Sexual history is often overlooked in medical and nursing home records. One home's admission form did not include a sexual history until a troubled eighty-two-year-old man wondered why nothing had been asked about his sex life. He said this was important to him and that he had been having some problems lately. After including a sexual history, the physician learned valuable information.

Are too many nursing home practices geared to institutional efficiency and the desires of the families rather than the patients themselves? Some activists have suggested that it should be possible to sue a nursing home for not allowing sexual activity; the suit would be based upon a violation of civil rights. Even if unsuccessful, such suits would serve to stimulate an awareness of the issues pertaining to patient rights. Until we have more advocates to make the concerns of nursing home residents highly visible, this probably will not happen. Nursing home residents tend, instead, to be among the most powerless, voiceless, and invisible groups in our country.

Many nursing home patients suffer from chronic anxiety, a condition that can be relieved by sexual orgasm. Enlightened staff and administrators of nursing homes, realizing the therapeutic value of sex, may knowingly turn their backs on clandestine sexual liaisons or solitary sexual behavior. A few actually encourage the activity. I asked one such person to comment about sexuality in his institution and he replied, "I just wish there was more of it." When I questioned him as to why there wasn't, he said it was mainly a problem for the staff.

Some nursing homes have set aside designated "petting rooms" where residents can go for privacy. This seems a little contrived, however, and I would suspect those who choose to go there would feel that all eyes are upon them and might expect to hear both staff and fellow residents say "We know where you're going!"

Beyond designating rooms for use by residents who desire to be intimate, some administrators have arranged for in-service education for the staff. I have had the opportunity to provide this in-service training at several nursing homes and can personally attest to the wide variety of feelings on the part of the staff. These feelings are a reflection of every social attitude. On one end are those who feel that whatever someone wants to do is perfectly all right with them, provided it is not hurting someone else. On the other end are the "protectors of us all," who feel it is their moral duty to control the behavior of others, based upon what *they* believe is right. I am certain the in-service provided much in the way of education, but probably did little to change the moral pronouncements of the participants. That was not my purpose. I was thrilled, though, to realize that administrators are beginning to see the need for an in-service dealing with sexuality. At least it is a beginning that could encourage other administrators to follow suit.

The next step, of course, should be patient education programs to discuss topics ranging from medical problems to atrophy resulting from sexual disuse. I could see this developing from an unstructured group setting that would lead eventually into discussions about sexuality after the group became comfortable with the leader. I think this would work better than starting right off talking about sex. Residents need to gain a better understanding and respect for the sexual needs of others. Often, I would suspect through jealousy, they condemn the actions of others or, like some staff, they are on the end of the continuum that says you must live by *my* moral standards. One staff member did mention that she considers the jealousy of other residents to be a primary inhibitor of sexual activity.

It is very probable that residents of nursing homes have a greater need than others for sexual intimacy. For those already suffering from a disability, emotional closeness can be of considerable benefit to their self-concept and self-esteem. Encouragement can be given in this area by helping residents to dress more attractively, thereby helping them to feel better about themselves. When residents feel better about themselves, they also feel better about each other. Even the reaction of staff to eye-appealing residents results in more time and attention being spent with them. The individual sense of masculinity and femininity is thus maintained and possibly enhanced.

Privacy is a serious problem. How would you feel if you were having sex with someone, or even just cuddling, and you knew that at any moment a staff member may be coming into your room, perhaps for a bed check or to administer medication? How much privacy is there when it is rare to have a private room? Almost all rooms provide a built-in roommate who may or may not feel like cooperating with your privacy needs. Take yourself out of the picture and substitute your mother or father instead. We expect them to accept what we know we wouldn't like ourselves. Would you like to have an unknown roommate forced upon you? Perhaps when you were in college that was all right. After all, you would only be there four years. But this roommate is for the rest of your mother's or father's life.

While you are still imagining your mother or father in a nursing home, or perhaps you have a parent who is already there, what reaction from staff might you expect if your parent were "caught" masturbating privately? There is a wide variety of reactions that might occur, depending upon the staff member. If the reaction is a negative one, such as patronizing, displaying anger, moralizing, teasing, or treating your parent like a child, this can lead to sexual inhibition and lowered self-esteem. The best reaction would be for the staff member to calmly excuse him- or herself and quietly close the door.

There is no doubt that staff members are faced with sexual behavior incidents in institutions, which even the most accepting of individuals have difficulty dealing with. A study by George Szasz of men in an extended care facility grouped these incidents into three broad categories: 1) sex talk, 2) sex acts, and 3) implied sexual behavior.[1]

The "sex talk" category included incidents in which residents used "foul language" to describe their past or present sexual experience and suggested that staff members enter into some form of sexual activity. An example was, "You wash me well, but what *else* can you do?"

The "sexual acts" category included incidents of residents exposing their genitalia, touching or grabbing the "private areas" of staff members, inappropriate removal of clothing, public masturbation, and, in one case, a resident was found engaging a prostitute behind the curtains of his bed.

Acts of "implied sexual behavior" included reading pornographic magazines, sexual comments about some actors and actresses on television, suggestive compliments, and requests for condom changes. Staff comments about this kind of behavior were especially negative when it took up their time, made it impossible to do their work, and made them avoid patient contact, not knowing how to refuse advances with tact or how to handle the situation.

Staff members do need to question themselves as to which of these upsetting activities would not be nearly so negative, nor hard to handle, if the suggestive comment and/or action had come from a younger person. The same comments and actions made by an older resident might be considered the prerogative of a younger patient. Yet these same remarks or actions are considered lecherous when delivered or conducted by an older person.

It must be remembered, too, that provocative sex acts may be a way to get attention and an opportunity to be touched, as clothes are put back on or changed, and the person is moved away from contact with another individual. Disturbing sexual behavior may be more the result of boredom, confusion, anger, or loneliness than lascivious intentions. The resident needs to be loved rather than punished. Punishment only adds to feelings of loneliness and depression.

Bernita M. Steffle suggests some staff guidelines that could be of help in institutions. What follows are questions that each administrator and staff member can ask him- or herself:[2]

1. If there is a problem related to sex, with whom is the problem associated? Patient? Staff? Family? What can I do about it?
2. Are physical problems that relate to sexuality well taken care of (e.g., senile vaginitis, catheters, and the like)?
3. Am I helping other staff members examine the meaning of the behavior of "the dirty old man" and "the shameless old woman"?
4. Am I aware of the isolation and sensory deprivation of the immobile patient?

Can I:

5. Provide opportunity for more touch (e.g., hugging, kissing, hand-holding) and intimacy such as back rubs and body massages?
6. Build sexuality into (rather than separate it from) the spiritual and emotional well-being of patients?
7. Accept and allow masturbation and help the staff to deal with it?
8. Provide more touching and feeling things to handle, fondle, and hold, such as yarn balls, prayer beads, and stuffed animals?
9. Bring life pets and allow patients to feel and cuddle them?
10. Provide more music: romantic, sentimental, sensuous, erotic?
11. Encourage opportunities for the sexes to meet, mingle, and spend time together, such as in small television rooms, without structuring a "trysting time or place" too rigidly?
12. Provide double beds for married couples?
13. Counsel families, particularly adult children of patients, about the sexual needs of older people?
14. Manipulate the environment to make the facility a therapeutic place?

And finally:

15. Do staff and patients laugh (and maybe cry) together?
16. Is there a Bill of Rights for sexual freedom in the facility?

I would like to comment briefly about number 9, the question about pets. Not only can this be beneficial to a nursing home resident, but the older person living alone has been shown to benefit greatly as well. Caring for, holding, and stroking a live pet enhances a person's sexuality through the touching and closeness that occurs. Just as we have found a significantly lower suicide rate among teenagers who have pets, so, too, the elderly benefit by having "someone" to talk to and care about. Study after study attests to the benefits. Pets have even "cured" aphasics (those who appear not to be able to speak or to understand the words of others). It must be remembered, however, that the death of a pet must be treated as a significant loss to the older person, perhaps equal to the loss of a special loved one.

The nursing home resident whom we usually picture is a woman. Not only is this the result of different life expectancy between men and women, but, since men die younger, they are usually ill at home and being taken care of by their wives. Thus when the wife becomes ill there is no husband at home anymore to help with care. The woman might need some assistance but not really that much. When I think of an older woman alone, I think of Minnie. She may be in a nursing home or she may be in her own home alone. Minnie was brought to life by the talented poet Donna Swanson. I challenge you to read her poem slowly and thoughtfully, as I have done for so many audiences.

*Minnie Remembers**

God; My hands are old.
I've never said that out loud
before but they are.
I was so proud of them once.
They were soft like the velvet
smoothness of a firm, ripe peach.
Now the softness is more like worn-
out sheets or withered leaves.
When did these slender, graceful
hands become gnarled,
shrunken claws? When, God?
They lie here in my lap,
naked reminders of this worn-out
body that has served me too well!

---

*"Minnie Remembers," by Donna Swanson, from *Mind Song*, published by Upper Room, Nashville, Tenn. For reprint call (317) 764-4225.

How long has it been since
someone touched me?
Twenty years?
Twenty years I've been a widow.
Respected. Smiled at.
But never touched.
Never held so close that
loneliness was blotted out.
I remember how my mother used
to hold me, God.
When I was hurt in spirit or flesh,
she would gather me close,
stroke my silky hair and caress
my back with her warm hands.
O God; I'm so lonely.
I remember the first boy who ever
kissed me.
We were both so new at that!
The taste of young lips and
popcorn, the feeling inside
of mysteries to come.
I remember Hank and the babies
How else can I remember them
but together?
Out of the fumbling, awkward
attempts of new lovers
came the babies.
And as they grew, so did our love
And, God, Hank didn't seem to
mind, if my body thickened
and faded a little.
He still loved it. And touched it.
And we didn't mind if we were no
longer beautiful.
And the children hugged me a lot.
O God, I'm lonely!
God, why didn't we raise the kids

to be silly and affectionate
as well as dignified and proper?
You see, they do their duty.
drive up in their fine cars:
they come to my room
to pay their respects.
They chatter brightly, and
reminisce.
But they don't touch me.
They call me "Mom" or "Mother"
or "Grandma."
Never Minnie.
My mother called me Minnie.
So did my friends.
Hank called me Minnie, too.
But they're gone.
And so is Minnie.
Only Grandma is here.
And God! She's lonely![3]

Just as Minnie remembers, so does "Peege." Have you seen that wonderful movie? I call it a classic in the field of aging. The story depicts Peege, an old woman, propped up in a chair in her nursing home room. Tubes are attached, her legs are swollen, her hands crippled by arthritis. Her family visits at Christmas and, as is so typical of families visiting nursing home residents, they too, sit stiffly in chairs or against the window sill, except for one grandson, Greg, the eldest. As the family chatters away meaninglessly, Greg sits close to Peege and in flashbacks, he remembers the Grandma he knew. Then, when the family leaves, he remains behind. With his arm around his grandma, his hand on hers, he reminisces with her. He allows her, in even her disabled condition, to feel the warmth of human touch and, as a result, to feel like a human being. After he leaves, the most beautiful smile I have ever seen, lights up her face and, at that moment, she experiences the sexuality that is part of her very personhood.

Maybe it is the young, such as Peege's grandson, who understand more the needs of the old. Maybe it's because the young and the old are not in control in this country; it is the middle-aged who have the power. The joining together of the old with the young, sometimes in programs such as I have developed that bring older volunteers into schools, allows for a beautiful exchange of love.

I asked my students, unburdened with the administrative details of running a nursing home, what they see as the sexual needs of the elders there. Some of them commented:

> "These people are not children who should be told what they can or cannot do. They are adults who should be able to decide if they want to pursue a sexual relationship."
>
> "Sex is something that should be addressed by the occupants living there, since it is considered their home."
>
> "Every nursing home should have a room that the residents could reserve for sexual purposes. Sex in a nursing home is okay but they need privacy. Also, respect is needed for those who don't participate."
>
> "Nursing homes should accommodate the need for privacy and intimacy just as other needs are provided for."
>
> "Sex in a nursing home is fine as long as it is done discretely like any other sexual relationship between two people is handled."
>
> "Sex in a nursing home is something that should be left to the choice of the individuals involved and never arbitrarily ruled on by staff or management. But I can see a problem with lack of privacy—and the feelings of residents who aren't having relationships would have to be considered."
>
> "Sex in a nursing home should be allowed just as it would be in any apartment, house, or other residence. That's their home and their rooms are *their* private place to do what they want."
>
> "Older people in nursing homes have another problem besides what society thinks of them as being old and sexless. They are worried about the staff judging them. Also, they might feel their sexual life is wrong since they have to sneak around."

One student who works in a nursing home spoke from personal experience:

"Sex in a nursing home is not widely accepted by staff *or* other residents. Mostly it is the other residents who object most strongly—jealousy?

A few semesters ago, two female residents from a nearby domicillary (or intermediate care facility) faithfully attended my human sexuality class. They took part in group discussions and, at ages sixty-five and ninety-two, exchanged stories with the other students. It was a wonderful growth experience for all. Toward the end of the semester, a local television newsman interviewed these two wonderful women for the six o'clock news. The ninety-two-year-old made us all smile when she said, "If I had known back when my husband was living what I know now, he would have been the happiest man alive." The other woman had never married but smiled knowingly. Let's hear it for sex education for all ages!

There is a film called "Rose By Any Other Name," which I recommend to family members of those in a nursing home, staff members and administrators of care facilities, and everyone concerned about older people. It depicts clearly the effects of the lack of closeness upon a resident who had been used to having Rose as a visitor to his room and a companion in his bed. Interestingly, it is Rose who gets in trouble with the administration. This is not unlike sexual situations at any age: the woman is *always* at "fault." Rose's daughter is called in, like a principal summoning a parent because her child got in trouble at school. At first Rose's daughter is upset with her mother, but then Rose poignantly asks, "Do we ever stop needing to be loved?" With her daughter's understanding now on her side, and realizing the anger and depression of her male friend, Rose once again enters his room. The film ends with a nurse summoning the administrator to the room. The viewer is left to ponder all too clearly what the consequences will be.

A friend and fellow gerontologist shared with me the story of her aunt, a resident in a local nursing home, for whom my friend had responsibility. In the early morning hours, my friend was awakened by the phone ringing. It was her aunt, asking her to come immediately. My friend asked what was wrong but her aunt continued to plead with her to "just come." Throwing on her clothes hurriedly, she jumped into the car, rushed to her aunt's room in the nursing home and guess what she found? There, in bed, was her aunt and her boyfriend, unable to extricate themselves from each other. His leg had gotten stuck in her garter! Is there sex in nursing homes? What do you think?

NOTES

1. George Szasz, "Sexual Incidents in an Extended Care Unit for Aged Men," *Journal for the American Geriatrics Society* 31 (July 1983): 407-11.

2. Bernita M. Steffle, "Sexuality and Aging: Implications for Nurses and Other Helping Professionals," in *Sexuality and Aging*, edited by Robert Solnick (Los Angeles: University of Southern California Press, 1978), 148-49.

3. Donna Swanson, "Minnie Remembers," in *Mind Song* (Nashville, Tenn.: Upper Room, 1978), 80.

11

Counseling Older Persons

What to Do When You Want to but Can't or You Can but Don't Want to

"Remember that people take more interest in their own affairs than in anything else which you can name. If you wish your conversation to be thoroughly agreeable, lead a mother to talk of her children, a young lady of her particular talent, an author of his forthcoming book, or an artist of his exhibition picture. Having furnished a subject, you need only listen, and you are sure to be thought not only agreeable, but thoroughly sensible and well-informed."

Eugenics, 1915

A fifty-nine-year-old man panics because, for the first time in his life, he just had a partial erection. Since he has misinformation about impotence, he becomes so anxious that he "psychs himself out" from having an erection the next time. His wife, equally misinformed, avoids coming to bed at night until he is asleep because she doesn't want to upset him. As a result, there is not only no intercourse, but no loving contact at all; suddenly there are two sexually deprived people, afraid to touch each other.

Here are two people whose lack of understanding of what can

happen to them sexually could mark an end to their intimate expressions. Will they seek counseling? Families may also need help and counseling regarding the sexuality of their older parents or grandparents. A counselor might act as a liaison to translate the needs of the older person to his or her family. Families may need help in accepting the drives and needs of an older family member. Will they consider it important enough to get this help?

I developed a workshop on sexuality and aging directed toward support persons, which was divided into seven weekly two-hour sessions. Methods of presentation included group and panel discussions, speakers, films, suggested readings, and printed materials distributed to each participant. The sessions were focused in the following areas:

Session I—Introduction and preview of sessions

Session II—Developmental stages: Physiological and Psychological

Session III—Societal influences: Religious, Cultural, and Generational

Session IV—Myths and facts of sexual aging

Session V—Institutionalized elders: Current problems and looking toward the future

Session VI—Handicapped and infirmed elders

Session VII—Counseling techniques: Understanding sexual needs

Workshop evaluations indicated that the participants felt much more comfortable and open in relation to sexual concerns of older persons and that a real need existed for this type of workshop. Attendance remained unusually high throughout. Many said, "Just put sex in the title!" A workshop such as this can be very beneficial since sexual problems can be one of the most common causes of feelings of helplessness among elders. Enlightened counseling could help them express and enjoy their natural sexuality. In spite of the openness with which sex has been discussed in recent years, there is still a need for professionals to be provided more information on aging in general, sexuality specifically, and counseling that combines the two. Counselors could be a key in encouraging aging males and females to continue an active sex life beyond the time that most are conditioned to think such activity "right" and/or "proper" or to help persons explore other ways to express their sexuality.

The old saying "You can't teach an old dog new tricks" has been proven to be absolutely wrong. Change can occur no matter what one's age, as long as the person is open and receptive. In fact, change should be encouraged. It is never too late to learn, especially if a person is willing to do the hard work of questioning, challenging, and ultimately getting rid of irrational beliefs.

Older couples can be helped if they recognize that normal age-related changes do exist, that they are not the same for the male and the female, and that each person reacts to changes in her or her special way. These changes are biological processes, none of which are produced by the quality of the couple's love or by their individual attractiveness. The presence of problems need not have any permanent effect on sexual functioning, provided they are discussed in an atmosphere of love, acceptance, and openness. Even the intimacy of intercourse can be set aside if individuals who are physically and spiritually close are able to find other ways to show tenderness, love, and respect for each other.

There are many things elders can do to understand and remedy sexual, personal, and social problems. Reading books and other related materials could be a starting point (see resource list at the end of this volume). Viewing films, attending lectures, taking part in workshops, all can be of benefit. Enrolling in a human sexuality class is a good idea. A course listing at local colleges and universities should help interested persons find the right class, most of which can be audited. Obtaining a thorough medical examination, and being willing to mention any sexual problems or concerns to the physician, is absolutely necessary. Physical problems can combine with social and emotional problems and eventually manifest themselves in a wide array of symptoms indicating sexual dysfunction. When problems persist, a counselor can be of tremendous help. Beyond his or her expertise in matters physical, a physician cannot be expected to offer advice; a counselor should step in here when psychological problems present themselves.

Counseling can be on an individual or group basis. Group counseling may be more conducive to exploration and sharing. In a group session members can support each other while exploring sensitive feelings. Older individuals, however, have not experienced groups as much as the youth of today. Therefore, they may well feel more comfortable with the privacy of individual counseling. For older persons who grew up at a time when schoolroom desks were bolted to the floor in straight lines, group work, especially in such delicate and personal matters, is not for them. Even individual therapy is difficult for those who grew up feeling that problems should not be discussed outside the home, certainly not sexual problems. In their day, it was not even appropriate to discuss sexual problems *within* the home.

Counselors also need to become more open to, and knowledgeable about, the problems of older persons. Many feel comfortable meeting with clients who are close to their age or younger because they can reflect on shared experiences. But when it comes to an older client, these counselors feel they lack the special understanding needed to advise an age group with whom they share few, if any, experiences. Besides, counseling persons old enough to be their parents or grandparents is scary and, they think, somewhat inappropriate. This puts them in a position of "child helping elder." Actually, it has been suggested that middle-aged to older counselors may, in fact, have the ability to express greater empathy and achieve more long-range success with older clients. It does seem unlikely that many older persons would find it possible to discuss their sexual matters with a twenty-five-year-old. It is important to remember that if a counselor is not the right one for you, it is perfectly all right to find someone more suitable to your needs. In fact, that is exactly what should be done rather than assuming you cannot be helped.

Older males who seek counseling may be experiencing a type of monotony brought on by being with the same partner or doing things the same way. If not yet retired, they may be preoccupied with their careers. Some may be experiencing mental or physical fatigue, physical infirmity or the disability of their partners. Perhaps overindulging in food or drink is the culprit. Then, of course, there is always the possibility of anxiety over performance—the old "fear of failure" syndrome. Some older persons may have become too inattentive to their own personal appearance, resulting in sloppiness, careless personal hygiene, or obesity. If not obese as such, some may find that the old pot belly may have become prominent. Here exercise and controlled diet are of paramount importance.

Since women have been so conditioned to equate desirability with youth and beauty, their responsiveness can be affected to the extent that they perceive themselves to be old and ugly. A counselor can't change the "old" but she (I would suggest a woman counselor here) can help an older woman to be more attractive through exercise and good grooming followed by working on her ability to *see* herself as attractive. Much of the decline in sexual interest among aging women is not physiologic but defensive. Many find it more adaptive to inhibit sexual strivings when little opportunity exists for sexual fulfillment.

It is important for older men and women to maintain or redevelop a pattern of sexual activity congruent with their own needs and with the aging process. There must be open and honest communication that is sensitive to the wishes of others. This includes the ability of each partner to verbalize his or her expectations. Each needs to explore avenues of sexual pleasure without intercourse and to consider alternate positions that are more effective for stimulating and maintaining an erection. They might try mutual masturbation as a variation on, or addition to, their "usual" lovemaking repertoire.

Counselors must be careful not to impose current cultural expectations upon older clients, a group who cannot be expected in any immediate way to overcome the sexual misapprehensions and taboos with which they have lived so long. It is important not to put someone in conflict with his or her own values by enforcing the counselor's personal morality and convictions. Since sexual performance in older persons is predicted by their performance throughout life, it must be kept in mind that for those older people who were not sexually active when young, a satisfactory involvement at another age may be far less active than for someone else, and yet every bit as satisfying.

Sexual therapy, since its inception, has been of a conjoint nature, the assumption being that there are two persons in need of counseling. In the case of older women, however, this type of therapy has no value for those who are alone. For this group, counseling to deal with aloneness is very much in order. Great sensitivity is required if such women are to be informed of the various options available (as discussed in chapter 6), and also helped to affirm themselves as women. They have been indoctrinated to feel that sex is dirty and bad, even sinful. Complaints of constipation or vague backache may actually be symptoms of their confusion over whether it is normal to have sexual feelings after age sixty, especially when a partner is no longer available.

Sexual issues frequently arise in counseling elders ostensibly while talking about other problems. It is, therefore, important for therapists to listen for, and ask about, the sexual concerns of their older clients. These elders will generally look on questions about their sexuality as compliments, since these are older adults who have been willing to come in for counseling. Those who do not want to talk about a personal matter just won't be there.

Case studies are interesting to read and to think about. I am including three that were reported on by Dr. Benjamin Liptzin, a psychiatrist.[1]

"Mr. J., a seventy-two-year-old man, was referred for psychiatric consultation because of excessive anxiety and difficulty in sleeping. His wife had lost interest in sex and ridiculed him as a "dirty old man" for retaining his interest, and used her advancing age to terminate a sexual relationship that had never been very gratifying to her. He became sexually aroused by a woman he met at a senior leisure group and was fearful that he might act on his impulses and that his wife might find out and humiliate him. He experienced some relief at reassurance that his sexual interest was not abnormal, but that he needed to weigh the risks of acting on his feelings against the benefits.

"Mr. K., a seventy-two-year-old man, had a very different dilemma that made him anxious. His wife of fifty years had grown up in the house next door to him as a youngster. When she died, he found himself aggressively pursued by several divorced or widowed women in his retirement community. He was bewildered by the changing sexual mores and the variety of sexual favors offered by what appeared to him to be "respectable" women. This was particularly difficult since he had never dated anyone other than his wife, who had been like a sister to him. His anxiety was reduced as he was able to sort out his wish for another companion or mother/sister figure from his excitement at these new experiences, which he had missed as an adolescent.

"Miss M. illustrates the problem created for some women by the prevailing culture, which exalts the sexual attractiveness of youth. This seventy-eight-year-old single woman came for counseling following the death of a sister with whom she lived. She came to the first interview wearing bright red lipstick, dyed blonde hair, and a short skirt. At first, her mode of relating was childlike and seductive. Despite her image of herself as a perpetual teenager, she was able to respond to attempts to help her confront her sadness over the loss of her sister and to allow herself to engage in senior citizen activities to combat her loneliness. Many women pursue cosmetic surgery, new wardrobes, and more desperate attempts to avoid accepting their aging selves, only to be disappointed."

Chapter 9 of this book discussed sexual problems that are health related. Along with information that needs to be shared regarding health or disability effects on sexuality, there are many practical ways to assist a couple. For the stroke victim, a football or trapeze will assist mobility. An arthritic may enjoy early morning sex preceded by a hot bath as part of foreplay to loosen joints. Those who complain that aspirin reduces sexual sensation should have sex *before* taking the medication. Use of a lubricant is most helpful for the woman who has reduced vaginal secretions. Don't bother taking an aphrodisiac: many older people (and younger ones as well) have tried this route, but the Food and Drug Administraiton has assured us that their claims of obtaining super-sexual status are sheer myth. So forget about wine, Spanish fly, Cayenne pepper, snakeroot, bloodroot, Vitamin E, and marijuana. The only true aphrodisiacs are good diet, good exercises, and a vivid imagination.

Sex should not be thought of as a prescription for what ails us, but rather as part of our total sexuality. Those who have developed a life style that does not include the first three letters in sexuality should not be made to feel guilty, as though they have not taken an essential vitamin. Likewise, those who have maintained sex as part of their total sexuality should feel society's acceptance of this as a very normal part of their lives. What elders need in order to feel sexual and sensual is an acceptance and love of their own bodies, a zest for life in general, and an appreciation of the sexuality and sensuality of others. Is that any different from what is needed at any age? Not a bit! Truly we are sexual beings from birth until death, and the more each generation realizes that, the less we will be able to say, or even think, "*MY* PARENTS NEVER HAD SEX!

NOTES

1. Benjamin Liptzin, "Clinical Perspectives on Sexuality in Older Patients," *Journal of Geriatric Psychiatry* 17 (1984): 167-81.

2. Domeena Renshaw, "Sex and the Senior Citizen," *Journal of the National Association of Private Psychiatric Hospitals* 10 (Fall 1978): 59.

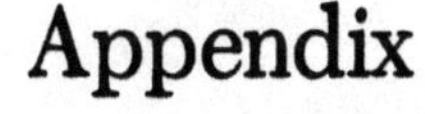

Appendix

Eight Reasons to Marry an Older Woman

Benjamin Franklin

1. Because they have more Knowledge of the world, and their Minds are better stored with Observations; their Conversation is more improving, and more lastingly agreeable.

2. Because when Women cease to be handsome, they study to be good. To maintain their Influence over Men, they supply the Diminution of Beauty by an Augmentation of Utility. They learn to do a thousand Services, small and great, and are the most tender and useful of all Friends when you are sick. Thus they continue amiable. And hence there is hardly such a thing to be found as an old Woman who is not a good Woman.

3. Because there is hazard of children, which irregularly produced may be attended with much inconvenience.

4. Because through more Experience they are more prudent and

From *Advice to a Young Man*, Philadelpohia, June 25, 1745.

discreet in conducting an Intrigue to prevent Suspicion. The Commerce with them is therefore safer with regard to your reputation, and with regard to theirs, if the Affair should happen to be known, considerate People might be rather inclined to excuse an old woman, who would kindly take care of a young Man, form his manners by her good Councils, and prevent his ruining his Health and Fortune among mercenary Prostitutes.

5. Because in every Animal that walks upright, the Deficiency of the Fluids that fill the Muscles appears first in the highest Part. The Face first grows lank and wrinkled; then the Neck; then the Breast and Arms; the lower parts continuing to the last as plump as ever; so that covering all above with a Basket, and regarding only what is below the Girdle, it is impossible of two Women to know an old one from a young one. And as in the Dark all Cats are gray, the Pleasure of Corporal Enjoyment with an old Woman is at least equal and frequently superior; every Knack being by Practice capable of improvement.

6. Because the sin is less. The Debauching of a Virgin may be her Ruin, and make her Life unhappy.

7. Because the Compunction is less. The having made a young Girl miserable may give you frequent bitter Reflections, none of which can attend making an old Woman happy.

8th & lastly. They are so grateful!!!

A Comparison of Sexual Response in Young and Aging Males

ERECTIVE ATTAINMENT	YOUNGER	OLDER
Excitement Phase	matter of seconds	matter of minutes —erection may not be as full or demanding —at plateau phase erection is established with security
	—testicular elevation	—little or none
	—deep vascular engorgement of testis	—little or none
Plateau Phase Period of intense sexual pleasure	—some pre-ejaculatory fluid emission from Cowper's glands	—markedly reduced
	—plateau phase short	—plateau phase can last indefinitely
Orgasmic Phase 1st stage ejaculatory inevitability man feels it coming and can no longer control it (2-4 sec.)		may be shortened, lengthened, or absent
2nd stage ejaculation	—12-36 in.	—force of expulsion diminished 3-12 in. does not interfere with man's sensate pleasure
Resolution Phase	—penis returns to flaccid state after minutes or hours	—returns in matter of seconds

Adapted from Masters, W. H. and Johnson, V. E., *Human Sexual Response* (Boston: Little Brown, 1966) by Clarice Lechner-Hyman and Elizabeth Kaiser, 1975.

A Comparison of Sexual Response in Young and Aging Females

	YOUNGER	OLDER
Excitement Phase	—vaginal lubrication occurs in 15-30 sec.	—delayed 1-4 min utes—if penile intromission is attempted before, can cause pain—even injury
	—vaginal vault on barrel expands potential space, corrugated sides (baby's head)	—degree to which barrel can expand is reduced—still sufficient for penile intromission
Plateau Phase	—uterus markedly enlarges—3 or 4 times	—enlargement decreases or may be absent
	—rises high into false pelvis	—may not rise at all
	—capable of multiple orgasms	—numbers of orgasms during one act of intercourse decreases
Orgasmic Phase	—10-12 contractions of uterus, muscles	—contractions decrease to
	vagina, perineum, and anus	
Resolution Phase	from 5 min. to hours	—markedly decreased

Adapted from Masters, W. H. and Johnson, V. E., *Human Sexual Response* (Boston: Little Brown, 1966) by Clarice Lechner-Hyman and Elizabeth Kaiser, 1975.

Aging Sexual Attitudes and Knowledge Scale

KNOWLEDGE QUESTIONS:
Correct answers are listed at the end of this section.

*1. Sexual activity in aged persons is often dangerous to their health.
   .1 True   .2 False   .3 Don't know

2. Males over the age of 65 typically take longer to attain an erection of their penis than do younger males.
   .1 True   .2 False   .3 Don't know

3. Males over the age of 65 usually experience a reduction in intensity of orgasm relative to younger males.
   .1 True   .2 False   .3 Don't know

4. The firmness of erection in aged males is often less than that of younger males.
   .1 True   .2 False   .3 Don't know

*Indicates that the scoring should be reversed such that 2 = 1, and 1 = 2, i.e., a low score indicates high knowledge.

From C. B. White, "A Scale for the Assessment of Attitude and Knowledge Regarding Sexuality in the Aged, "*Archives of Sexual Behavior*" 11 (1982): 491-502.

5. The older female (65+ years of age) has reduced vaginal lubrication secretion relative to younger females.
.1 True .2 False .3 Don't know

6. The aged female takes longer to achieve adequate vaginal lubrication relative to younger females.
.1 True .2 False .3 Don't know

7. The older female may experience painful intercourse due to reduced elasticity of the vagina and reduced vaginal lubrication.
.1 True .2 False .3 Don't know

8. Sexuality is typically a life-long need.
.1 True .2 False .3 Don't know

9. Sexual behavior in older people (65+) increases the risk of heart attack.
.1 True .2 False .3 Don't know

*10. Most males over the age of 65 are unable to engage in sexual intercourse.
.1 True .2 False .3 Don't know

11. Relatively speaking, the most sexually active younger people tend to become the most sexually active older people.
.1 True .2 False .3 Don't know

12. There is evidence that sexual activity in older persons has beneficial physical effects on the participants.
.1 True .2 False .3 Don't know

13. Sexual activity may be psychologically beneficial to older person participants.
.1 True .2 False .3 Don't know

*14. Most older females are sexually unresponsive.
.1 True .2 False .3 Don't know

15. The sex urge typically increases with age in males over 65.
    .1 True .2 False .3 Don't know

16. Prescription drugs may alter a person's sex drive.
    .1 True .2 False .3 Don't know

17. Females, after menopause, have a physiologically induced need for sexual activity.
    .1 True .2 False .3 Don't know

18. Basically, changes with advanced age (65+) in sexuality involve a slowing of response time rather than a reduction of interest in sex.
    .1 True .2 False .3 Don't know

19. Older males typically experience a reduced need to ejaculate and maintain an erection of the penis for a longer time than younger males.
    .1 True .2 False .3 Don't know

*20. Older males and females cannot act as sex partners as both need younger partners for stimulation.
    .1 True .2 False .3 Don't know

21. The most common determinant of the frequency of sexual activity in older couples is the interest or lack of interest of the husband in a sexual relationship with his wife.
    .1 True .2 False .3 Don't know

22. Barbiturates, tranquilizers, and alcohol may lower the sexual arousal levels of aged persons and interfere with sexual responsiveness.
    .1 True .2 False .3 Don't know

23. Sexual disinterest in aged persons may be a reflection of a psychological state of depression.
    .1 True .2 False .3 Don't know

24. There is a decrease in frequency of sexual activity with older age in males.
.1 True .2 False .3 Don't know

25. There is a greater decrease in male sexuality with age than there is in female sexuality.
.1 True .2 False .3 Don't know

26. Heavy consumption of cigarettes may diminish sexual desire.
.1 True .2 False .3 Don't know

27. An important factor in the maintenance of sexual responsiveness in the aging male is the consistency of sexual activity throughout his life.
.1 True .2 False .3 Don't know

28. Fear of the inability to perform sexually may bring about an inability to perform sexually in older males.
.1 True .2 False .3 Don't know

29. The ending of sexual activity in old age is most likely and primarily due to social and psychological causes rather than biological and physical causes.
.1 True .2 False .3 Don't know

*30. Excessive masturbation may bring about an early onset of mental confusion and dementia in the aged.
.1 True .2 False .3 Don't know

*31. There is an inevitable loss of sexual satisfaction in post-menopausal women.
.1 True .2 False .3 Don't know

32. Secondary (or non-physiologically caused) impotence increases in males over the age of 60 relative to younger males.
.1 True .2 False .3 Don't know

33. Impotence in aged males may literally be effectively treated and cured in many instances.
    .1 True .2 False .3 Don't know

34. In the absence of severe physical disability males and females may maintain sexual interest and activity well into their 80s and 90s.
    .1 True .2 False .3 Don't know

35. Masturbation in older males and females has beneficial effects on the maintenance of sexual responsiveness.
    .1 True .2 False .3 Don't know

ANSWERS: 1. False, 2. True, 3. True, 4. True, 5. True, 6. True, 7. True, 8. True, 9. False, 10. False, 11. True, 12. True, 13. True, 14. False, 15. False, 16. True, 17. False, 18. True, 19. True, 20. False, 21. True, 22. True, 23. True, 24. True, 25. True, 26. True, 27. True, 28. True, 29. True, 30. False, 31. False, 32. True, 33. True, 34. True, 35. True.

\+ ATTITUDE QUESTIONS: (Seven point Likert Scale, Disagree = 1, Agree = 7)
Disagree 1—2—3—4—5—6—7 Agree

The following statements test your attitudes. No answers are provided:

36. Aged people have little interest in sexuality. (Aged = 65+ years of age). ________

37. An aged person who shows sexual interest brings disgrace to himself/herself. ________

38. Institutions, such as nursing homes, ought not to encourage or support sexual activity of any sort in its residents. ________

39. Male and female residents of nursing homes ought to live on separate floors or separate wings of the nursing home. ________

40. Nursing homes have no obligation to provide adequate privacy for residents who desire to be alone, either by themselves or as a couple. ________

41. As one becomes older (say past 65) interest in sexuality inevitably disappears. ________

For items 42, 43, and 44:
If an elderly relative of mine, living in a nursing home, was to have a sexual relationship with another resident, I would:

42. Complain to the management. ________

43. Move my relative from this institution. ________

+44. Stay out of it as it is not my concern. ________

45. If I knew that a particular nursing home permitted and supported sexual activity in residents who desired such, I would not place a relative in that nursing home. ________

46. It is immoral for older persons to engage in recreational sex. ________

+47. I would like to know more about the changes in sexual functioning in the older years. ________

+48. I feel I know all I need to know about sexuality in the aged. ________

49. I would complain to the management if I knew of sexual activity between any residents of a nursing home. ________

+50. I would support sex education courses for aged residents of nursing homes. ________

+51. I would support sex education classes for the staff of nursing homes. ________

+52. Masturbation is an acceptable sexual activity for older males. ________

+53. Masturbation is an acceptable sexual activity for older females. ________

+54. Institutions, such as the nursing home, ought to provide large enough beds for couples who desire such to sleep together. ________

+55. Staff of nursing homes ought to be trained or educated with regard to sexuality in the aged and/or disabled. ________

56. Residents of nursing homes ought not to engage in sexual activity of any sort. ________

+57. Institutions, such as nursing homes, should provide opportunities for the social interaction of men and women. ________

58. Masturbation is harmful and ought to be avoided. ________

+59. Institutions, such as nursing homes, should provide privacy such as to allow the residents to engage in sexual behavior without fear of intrusion or observation. ________

60. If family members object to a widowed relative engaging in sexual relations with another resident of a nursing home, it is the obligation of the management and staff to make certain that such sexual activity is prevented. ________

61. Sexual relations outside the context of marriage are always wrong. ________

+Reverse scoring on items indicated such that 1 = 7, 7 = 1; 6 = 2, 2 = 6; 3 = 5, 5 = 3; 4 unchanged. A low score indictes a permissive attitude.

Resources

PUBLICATIONS

General

Anderson, Barbara G. *The Aging Game: Success, Sanity, and Sex After Sixty*. New York: McGraw-Hill, 1980.

Botwin, Carol. *Is There Sex After Marriage?* Boston: Little Brown and Co., 1985.

Brecher, Edward M., and the editors of Consumer Report Books. *Love, Sex and Aging*. Boston: Little Brown and Co., 1984.

Butler, Robert N. and Myrna I. Lewis. *Sex After Sixty: A Guide for Men and Women for Their Later Years*. New York: Harper and Row, 1976.

Comfort, Alex. *The Joy of Sex*. New York: Crown, 1976.

Partnow, Elaine. *Breaking the Age Barrier*. New York: Pinnacle Books, 1981.

Sheehy, Gail. *Passages: Predictable Crises of Adult Life*. New York: Bantam Books, 1973.

Solnick, Robert L., ed. *Sexuality and Aging*. Los Angeles: The University of Southern California Press, 1978.

Starr, B. D. and M. B. Weiner. *Sex and Sexuality in the Mature Years*. New York: Stein and Day, 1981.

Weg, Ruth B., ed. *Sexuality in the Later Years*. Orlando, Fla.: Academic Press, 1983.

Counseling

Capuzzi, Dave. "Sexuality and Aging: An Overview for Counselors," *Personnel and Guidance Journal* 61 (September 1982): 31-35.

Hammond, Doris and Jack M. Sink, "Myths and Realities of Sexual Aging: Implications for Counseling," *Counseling and Values* 24 (April 1980): 155-165.

Health

Arthritis Foundation. *Living and Loving: Information About Sex*. Atlanta, Ga.: Arthritis Foundation, 1982.

Impotence Information Center. *Impotence After Cancer Surgery*. American Medical Systems, P.O. Box 9, Minneapolis, MN 55440.

Professional Self-Help Aids Catalog. Brookfield, Ill.: Fred, Sammons, 1984. (Includes safety and personal care products.)

Robmault, Isabel P. *Sex, Society and the Disabled*. New York: Harper and Row, 1978.

Schiengold, L. D. and N. W. Wagner. *Sound Sex and the Aging Heart*. New York: Human Sciences Press, 1974.

Ulery, Barbara. *Sex and Dialysis*. (May be ordered by sending $3.75 to Barbara Ulery, P.O. Box 462, Durango, CO 81301.)

Walz, Thomas H. and Nancee S. Blum. *Sexual Health in Later Life*. Lexington, Mass.: D. C. Heath and Co., 1987.

Homosexuality

Berger, Robert M. *Gay and Gray: The Older Homosexual Man.* Urbana, Ill.: University of Illinois Press, 1982.

Men

Levinson, Daniel J. *The Seasons of a Man's Life.* New York: Alfred A. Knopf, 1978.

Pesman, C. and the editors of *Esquire. How a Man Ages.* New York: Ballentine Books, 1984.

Menopause

Triem, Susan Flamholtz. *Changes of Life.* New York: Fawcett Columbine, 1986.

Nursing Homes

Bowker, L. H. *Humanizing Institutions for the Aged.* Lexington, Mass.: Lexington Books, 1982.

Fox, Nancy. *You, Your Parent and the Nursing Home.* Buffalo, N.Y.: Prometheus Books, 1986.

Women

Loewinsohn, R. J. *Survival Handbook for Widows (and for Relatives and Friends Who Want to Understand).* American Association of Retired Persons (AARP). Glenview, Ill.: Scott, Foresman, 1984.

Porcino, Jane. *Growing Older, Getting Better: A Handbook for Women in the Second Half of Their Life.* Reading, Mass.: Addison-Wesley Publishing Co., 1983.

AUDIO-VISUAL

Minnie Remembers (5 min. color)

Produced by Mass Media Ministries
2116 N. Charles Street
Baltimore, MD 21218

Available from the audio-visual departments of the following universities:

Central Washington University

Iowa State University

North Texas State University

University of Minnesota

University of Missouri

University of Wisconsin, Madison

Washington State University

The Massey Tapes: *What You Are Is What You Were When*

Magnetic Video Library
23705 Industrial Park Drive
Farmington Hills, MI 48024
(313) 477-6066

Peege

It may be rented for $15.50 plus UPS charge from:
University Film and Video
University of Minnesota
1313 5th Street, S.E.
Minneapolis, MN 55414
(800) 847-8251.

Rose by Any Other Name

Adelphi University Center on Aging
Garden City, NY 11530
(516) 486-4530

It may be rented for $15.50 plus UPS charges from:
University Film and Video
University of Minnesota
1313 5th Street, S.E.
Minneapolis, MN 55414
(800) 847-8251

ORGANIZATIONS

American Association for Counseling and Development (AACD)
5999 Stevenson Ave.
Alexandria, VA 22304.
(703) 823-9800

American Association of Sex Educators, Counselors, and Therapists
5010 Wisconsin Avenue, N.W.
Suite 304
Washington, DC 20016

A booklet is available listing counselors, therapists and educators by location.

National Cancer Institute
Cancer Information Service (CIS)
Toll Free number: 1-800-4-cancer

Senior Action in a Gay Environment (SAGE)
P.O. Box 115
New York, NY 10023
Referral can be made to a similar organization near you.

Sex Information and Education Council of the United States (SIECUS)
84 Fifth Avenue
New York, NY 10010

Understanding Aging, Inc. (An organization dedicated to intergenerational concerns, activities, and networking.)
Center for Understanding Aging
Framingham State College
Framingham, MA 01701
(617) 626-4979

United Ostomy Association, Inc.
2001 W. Beverly Boulevard
Los Angeles, CA 90057

Your local county's Office of Senior Services can make referrals depending upon your needs.

www.ingramcontent.com/pod-product-compliance
Lightning Source LLC
Chambersburg PA
CBHW021827020426
42334CB00014B/526

* 9 7 8 0 8 7 9 7 5 4 1 3 6 *